W9-AHJ-838

THE HIDDEN WEB

THE HIDDEN WEB

A *Sourcebook*

William O. Scheeren

LIBRARIES UNLIMITED

AN IMPRINT OF ABC-CLIO, LLC
Santa Barbara, California • Denver, Colorado • Oxford, England

Library of Congress Cataloging-in-Publication Data

Scheeren, William O.
    The hidden Web : a sourcebook / William O. Scheeren.
        pages cm
    Includes bibliographical references and index.
        ISBN 978–1–59884–627–0 (pbk.) — ISBN 978–1–59884–628–7 (ebook) 1. Invisible Web.
2. Internet addresses—Directories. 3. Internet searching. 4. Database searching. 5. Internet in school libraries. I. Title.
    ZA4237.S34   2012
    025.042′2—dc23   2011042977

ISBN: 978–1–59884–627–0
EISBN: 978–1–59884–628–7

16 15 14 13 12   1 2 3 4 5

This book is also available on the World Wide Web as an eBook.
Visit www.abc-clio.com for details.

Libraries Unlimited
An Imprint of ABC-CLIO, LLC

ABC-CLIO, LLC
130 Cremona Drive, P.O. Box 1911
Santa Barbara, California 93116-1911

This book is printed on acid-free paper ∞

Manufactured in the United States of America

Contents

1

What Is the Invisible Web and Why Is It Important to Librarians?

Throughout my years as a school librarian, the biggest challenge faced by both my students and I was finding the best information that most specifically answered their research questions. Prior to the proliferation of the Internet and other electronic resources, it was easier to locate information in the school library because it was either in the library or it was not. If the information was in the library, the students and I could easily locate it; if it was not in the library, there were relatively few alternatives as to how to obtain the information. Some libraries were members of a consortium or had cooperative agreements for inter-library loan; some of these welcomed school libraries into their membership. If you were fortunate enough to be in an area that had college or large public libraries, students were generally welcome to use the facilities, albeit with many restrictions such as not being allowed to borrow materials. The reality was that often these opportunities were not available for reasons of time and distance.

The move to electronic resources in school libraries was slower than for public and academic libraries especially when they served a larger clientele and had larger budgets. The use of electronic resources in schools can be traced on a continuum beginning with the use of commercial databases such as LexusNexis, Orbit, and Dialog. Using these databases was a real breakthrough in information gathering, but they were just the initial steps towards where we are now. First, for many school districts these databases were prohibitively expensive. They were subscription services, but in addition to the subscription price, they also charged by the search. Second, both because of the cost and the complexity of the search process, the searching had to be done by the librarian. No school district was going to pay the fees involved with the databases and allow students to search or browse indiscriminately. Certainly, the use of these subscription databases was a step forward in the information gathering process. However, they still remained very expensive for individual schools to purchase and if the school district was small, buying a license for a database remained very expensive.

One of the solutions for the use of databases in every school came about when states began to use state funds to purchase databases for use in every library within the state. However, this type of resource was limited to the states whose legislators would fund such purchases. Training was also something that needed to be shared with librarians within the state so that they could teach their patrons how to access the databases. This opportunity became a starting point for many students who could access these databases while they were in school or if they went to their public libraries, even if they did not have access to a computer at home.

For national access to information, it was the introduction and the proliferation of the Internet and the World Wide Web (WWW) that changed information-gathering behavior forever in school libraries as well as in other types of libraries. It is impossible to overstate how important the Internet has been to libraries, to librarians, and to students. Who among us does not remember our early experiences with the Internet: Dial-up modems, terminal-like screen displays, and really limited amounts of data? There was even a modicum of humor as we did Gopher searches through the main "Gopher Hole" at the University of Minnesota, whose athletic teams are known as the "Golden Gophers." The reality was, however, that we, as school librarians, had a very powerful way to access and deliver information to our clients. Unfortunately, we did not have a clue or even a suspicion how to use it effectively at the time.

Let us move forward to the school library of the twenty-first century. Technology has completely changed what we do. The computer has become more and more powerful and less and less expensive. Students and librarians are adept at finding exactly the information they need by searching the Internet. Or are they as adept as we think (and hope!)? Ask students and teachers how they search for and locate information on the Internet and the overwhelming answer is that they use a search engine. Furthermore, many users are such basic searchers that the search engines often return 10,000,000 or more results, many of which turn out to be irrelevant to their information needs.

Even the most sophisticated searcher, no matter what search engine they use, is only touching the surface of the information available on the Internet because they are not able to search the Invisible Web. The Invisible Web is also known as the Deep Web, Deepnet, or the Hidden Web. The Invisible Web contains information that cannot be accessed by general purpose search engines such as Google (Devine and Egger-Sider, 2009, p. 3). Several authors have compared the use of today's search engines that search for information on the Internet to fishing trawlers who trawl for fish on or near the surface of the ocean. They get a lot of information but are just touching the surface of what is out there. The terminology or concept of the Invisible Web has been in existence for over 15 years, but it is still little known by students or librarians.

In an informal survey of my students in a master's degree program, I asked how they search for information on the Internet. The vast majority of them said they used broad search terms in a general purpose search engine. A few stated they used search limiters when using the general search engines and also made use of the college's subscription databases. None of my students had even heard of the Invisible Web. When I explained the type of information that could be found on the Internet, they agreed unanimously that they could not understand why they did not know about it. Unfortunately, many librarians are as unaware of the Invisible Web and what it contains as are my students.

Before we proceed with a general discussion of what is contained in the Invisible Web, we need to establish that the Invisible Web is far, far larger than the Visible Web. I could provide some numbers about the size of the Internet and about how many Web sites exist, but that information would be out-of-date as soon as I put the numbers on the page. What we do know is that there are billions of Web sites in existence and that for every Web site that can be accessed using a standard search engine such as Google, there are five to ten that exist on the Invisible Web and cannot be located using basic search engines. Furthermore, the Invisible Web is growing at a far greater rate than is the Visible Web (Devine and Egger-Sider, 2009, p. xxi).

That now brings us around to a general discussion and description of what types of information are contained in the Invisible Web. All users should keep in mind, however, that while some items may be invisible using certain search engines, they may be part of the Visible Web because other search engines can locate them (Sherman and Price, 2007, p. 84). In general, though, the following types of items are only accessible through the Invisible Web (Devine and Egger-Sider, 2009, pp. 3 and 9).

1. Database Content. One would suppose that this would be part of the Visible Web, but search engines have almost no success locating database content because they are dynamically generated by querying the database. It is impossible to replicate that type of search either by using a general search engine or by entering the URL for the search results page in a browser because results were dynamically generated and then, the search form was reset. In other words, a search for information such as comparisons of literacy rates among countries is created by dynamically generated HTML pages that cannot be recreated without using the original database.
2. Deep Web Sites. This category sounds as though we are talking in riddles, but sites known as Deep Web sites generally are so data intensive that search engines such as Yahoo and Google cannot find their information.

3. As a general rule, some file formats cannot be located using standard search engines. This category includes any non-HTML formats. This will be discussed in more depth in Chapter 3, What Is in the Invisible Web, Can It Be Searched, and Why Use the Invisible Web?
4. Forms. This is closely related to the database results discussed above. Forms normally reset once the form is completed and submitted and therefore, even using the URL of the form in your browser before it is submitted will be unsuccessful. This again has to do with the dynamic content of forms.
5. Very Current Material. The most current information is often not available through standard search engines because the vast amount of this current information is often beyond the ability of most standard search engines to assimilate and index it.
6. Ephemeral Information. In contrast to information that remains on the Internet for what seems to be forever is ephemeral information. This is information that is either time-sensitive or so short-lived that standard search engines never have it available.
7. Gray Literature. This is a category of non-technical government information that is rarely found using standard search engines and resides on this enormous Invisible Web.

The last issue addressed in this chapter is why the Invisible Web should matter to librarians. In reality, the answer to this is far simpler than finding information on the Invisible Web: it allows librarians and students to find the best, most precise information and data that suits their information needs. It is up to the librarian to learn what is available on the Invisible Web and be prepared to share this knowledge with faculty so that they can encourage its use with their students. It is also important that librarians help students use the Invisible Web when they have a reference question or a research assignment which requires the information found there.

2

How Search Engines Work (or Do Not Work) with the Invisible Web

In Chapter 1, the concept that material in the Invisible Web cannot generally be accessed or retrieved using standard search engines such a Google or Yahoo was discussed. Keep in mind, however, that not all search engines return the same things as others even when the exact same search is done. Furthermore, meta search engines such as Dogpile use multiple search engines to search the Internet and return extremely comprehensive hit lists. What all of this means is that if you search "Shakespeare" in Yahoo, Google, and Dogpile, each search engine will have many of the same results, but there will be differences in the results lists for each of the three search engines.

It is perhaps important to note that general or standard search engines will not find material in the Invisible Web, and it cannot be found for two reasons. First, as powerful as many search engines are, they have technology limitations that prevent them from getting to the Invisible Web. Second, it is extremely expensive to develop and maintain comprehensive, general purpose search engines. Those search engines look at literally billions of Web sites and attempt to organize them into some manageable whole. It is just not financially practical, therefore, for a comprehensive general purpose search engine to delve into the Invisible Web even if it could (Sherman and Price, 2007, p. xiii).

Let's now reexamine the types of files that are typically not found by standard search engines and are therefore a part of the Invisible Web. In general, search engines do not "play well" with material that is not text-based. Web pages that are primarily video, audio, or images—in other words non-text-based material—are rarely accessible through the standard search engine. There are some specific files formats within these general file types that search engines cannot handle. These are:

- PDF or Postscript formats unless they come from Google.
- Flash. Of course, Apple and iPads also have issues with this file format.
- Shockwave.
- Programs. Actually all executable files.
- Compressed files such as .zip files.

The difficulty with indexing these types of files is that they are not HTML text and standard search engines generally do not choose to index them, mostly for financial reasons (Sherman and Price, 2007, p. 58).

In the larger picture, these types of files make up a small percentage of the material found in the Invisible Web. The much larger amount of material found on the Invisible Web is one of two types: (1) single Web pages or (2) database information. Single Web pages are generally Web pages created by individual users. The information contained on these Web pages is sometimes valuable, but they cannot be located by standard search engines because there are no links for the Web crawlers that are at the heart of search engines to locate the page.

The second large category of material located on the Invisible Web is database information which can generally be further divided into three categories. The first is database material that is designed for the needs of individual users. This data is often generated by forms and is contained in relational databases. Standard Web search engines cannot fill out the required information in interactive forms and therefore, even if you have an exact URL of the search, it will not return the data. The second type of data found in databases in the Invisible Web is streaming or real-time content. Because there is so much of it and it changes so rapidly, standard Web search engines just cannot keep up with this content. The third type is dynamically generated content. This is similar to the first item discussed relative to database information on the Invisible Web (Sherman and Price, 2007, p. 60-61).

Throughout this chapter we have considered why search engines cannot *access* material that is contained in the Invisible Web, but we have not discussed the technical aspects of how search engines *find* material on the Web. Most people do not need to know much more than how to enter a search term in a search engine; the search engine searches the Web and then produces a results list of Web sites that the search engine has determined meet the search criteria. This is a gross oversimplification, however. If it were that easy, then simple searches would always be sufficient. Let's now consider some problems (shortcomings) noted with general purpose search engines. These problems can be categorized into three general areas: (1) retrieval limits, (2) search strategy problems, and (3) evaluation issues.

RETRIEVAL LIMITS

1. The Web simply has too much material for any one search engine to find and index everything. Tough decisions have to be made both from a practical and a financial standpoint. It goes without saying that sometimes the information you want is not indexed and is therefore not available on the Visible Web.
2. Much of the information returned in a result list is irrelevant to the searcher. Why does this occur? It occurs generally because of poor or inexact search strings. For example, if a searcher is interested in material about William Shakespeare and enters the search term "Shakespeare," not only will the results list have information about William Shakespeare, but also about Shakespeare fishing equipment, Shakespeare festivals, etc.
3. Again, there are the search engine limitations that have been discussed earlier in this chapter. It is not technically or financially feasible to design or create a search engine that finds everything on every topic every time.
4. People do not realize that everything on the Web is not free. When the author was working as a school librarian and the Web was in its infancy, a member of our board of school directors stated that there would soon be no need for brick-and-mortar school libraries because everything was on the Web and it was all free. Sadly, this has not proved to be true.

SEARCH STRATEGY PROBLEMS

1. Poor search skills are closely related to item two above: irrelevant data or result lists. If searchers are not trained in search skills, often the result list will not be relevant. Training users in search skills is a key part of information literacy instruction for school librarians.
2. Nearly all search engine users consider themselves to be advanced or experienced searchers. The reality is that few are experienced or diligent enough searchers to take advantage of such advanced search engine features as Boolean Operators or search limiters.
3. Some searchers always use the same search engine. While this develops a certain amount of skill in searching, it ignores the fact that different search engines almost always return different result lists. Routinely using a meta search engine can alleviate this issue to some degree.
4. Again related to several items that have been discussed previously, many searchers do the simplest kind of searches. In our previous example of Shakespeare, this is an example of a simple search. A more sophisticated searcher might try to limit the search terms and use Boolean search limits.
5. Psychological studies have shown that Web users have a distinct aversion to scrolling through multiple screen result lists. When a result list returns many (perhaps even thousands) of result screens, it is almost inevitable that some useful results will be missed.

6. As a corollary of item five, there is often a high level of frustration when viewing numerous links to material. It often becomes overwhelming to the searcher.
7. Some of the value of items found on a result list lessens when there are thousands or millions of results.
8. Searchers are impatient people as witness the studies that show they are not willing to scroll through several pages of a results list. After a certain point, they just feel they are wasting time.
9. Searchers often do not use the Help feature of the search engine. This is generally the easiest, most accessible assistance and most searchers ignore it.
10. Quality sites are returned in searchers' result lists. Often however, searchers are more impressed with the volume of information on a site rather than the quality of the information.

EVALUATION ISSUES

1. General search engines do not evaluate the information that is returned in results lists. It is incumbent of the searcher to determine what is the best information.
2. Many, in fact most commercial Web sites contain advertising. After all, this is how many Web sites are paid for. Unfortunately, general search engines see this advertising and will include them in result lists. This is how information about Shakespeare fishing equipment becomes intermixed with information about William Shakespeare.
3. Tons of inappropriate sites are out there on the Web. Web search engines often pick them up (Devine and Egger-Sider, 2009, p. 29–31).

The final topic that will be discussed in this chapter is a series of what might be called Web searching myths. These are items that most people believe to be true but are, in fact, false.

1. Everything worth finding is already on the Web. If it can't be found on the Web, it is not worth finding. This is obviously not true. If it were true there would be need to update Web sites or to create new Web sites.
2. Google and other general search engines search the entire Web. We already know this is not correct or there would be no such thing as the Invisible Web. The Invisible Web contains at least 500 times as much material as the Visible Web.
3. The best information is in the first ten results. As mentioned above search engines do not rate results in any way. Therefore, it follows that there can be no hard and fast rule that the best material is in the first ten items of a result list.

4. Searching is easy. This can be true, but good searching is hard. Anyone can type in a search term but it takes skill to construct a search string that returns what the searcher needs.
5. Everything important on the Web is free. How many ways can we say no to this? In fact, the best material is often in subscription databases.
6. Everything on the Web is truthful, authentic, and accurate. Suffice to say that anyone can post anything to the Web at any time. (Devine and Egger-Sider, 2009, p. 4).

3

What Is in the Invisible Web, Can the Invisible Web Be Searched, and Why Use the Invisible Web?

Chapters 1 and 2 examined what the Invisible Web is, why the Invisible Web is a valuable resource for the school librarian, and how search engines do or do not work with the Invisible Web. In Chapter 3, the final chapter before we move to the chapters that deal specifically with Invisible Web sites of value to school librarians, we will take a more in-depth look at (1) what is in the Invisible Web, (2) determining if the Invisible Web can be searched, and, the biggest question of all, (3) why we should use the Invisible Web. In addition, we will examine what are considered to be the most useful Invisible Web categories. Finally, we will enumerate what cannot be found on the Web, using either the Visible or the Invisible Web.

The second question mentioned above is the one that will be answered first: can the Invisible Web be searched? At the gross level, the answer is "no." Basic search engines such as Google and Yahoo can locate Invisible Web tools, but they are not able to extract information from these tools (Devine and Egger-Sider, 2009, p. 147). The basic search engine is able to get to an Invisible Web tool such as a database containing census information, but you are not able to mine this information directly from the database using the basic search engine. You must go to the database on the Invisible Web to mine for and extract specific information.

The Visible Web is also known as the Surface Web. If we go back to the analogy of accessing the Visible Web as like trawling the ocean for fish at a shallow depth, then the term "Surface Web" becomes obvious. If we go back also to our discussion about what is in the Invisible Web—single Web pages, databases, current information, and forms—we can then compare the contents of the Surface Web with those of the Invisible Web. Bear in mind that the figures quoted in the next paragraph will be more than a year old by the time this book is published, so there certainly are more items in both the Visible Web and the Invisible Web as you read this book!

First, it is estimated that there are 71 billion static Web pages available on the World Wide Web. Of this number, only about 12.5 billion public Web pages are indexed by Google. So, what does that leave for the Invisible Web? First, there are an estimated 6.5 billion Web pages that are hidden from the public. Second, and far more significant, there are more than 220 billion database-driven Web pages that are invisible to Web search engines such as Google (Devine and Egger-Sider, 2009, p. 112). These figures, above all, point out the vast amount of material available in the Invisible Web.

As a general rule, there are two different types of sites on the Web. The first type are sites that provide content to the Web user. For the most part, these fall on the Invisible Web. The second type of sites are those that provide for easier Web navigation and allow users to discover resources (Sherman and Price, 2007, p. 78). Beyond that, Web users must be aware that sites may have either direct or indirect URLs. A direct URL takes the user directly to a specific Web page, such as http://www.pitt.edu. An indirect URL points to information that is executed by a script on a server. This is the core of using databases on the Invisible Web (Sherman and Price, 2007, p. 79).

Perhaps it only confuses the issue, but within the Invisible Web there are different types, or levels, of invisibility. Working from the opaque downward, the higher the level, the more likely the site may be indexed by a search engine such as Google. At the highest, or least invisible level, is the Opaque Web. Sites in the Opaque Web may be visible to search engines because of:

- Their depth of content; the more the content the less likely it will be in the Visible Web.
- The frequency of the search engine's crawl; this is particularly true for content that changes frequently.
- A limit in Web search engines of the number of receivable results.
- The presence of disconnected URLs and stand-alone Web pages.

The second level of invisibility is what is known as the Private Web. This part of the Invisible Web includes the following:

- Web sites that require passwords, such as subscription databases.
- Robots.txt that do not allow spider searching by search engines.
- "Noindex" meta tags in the Web page's HTML code.

The third level of Invisible Web sites are those that are part of the Proprietary Web. This may include Web sites that either require a registration (generally free) or are fee-based. The final level of invisibility contains those sites that are truly invisible and are never available to search engines (Sherman and Price, 2007, pp. 70–75).

Before moving to a list of the most popular Invisible Web categories, let's examine the final question in the Chapter 13 title, why and when to use the Invisible Web. In general terms, there are five basic reasons why searchers and school librarians should use the Invisible Web.

1. When the searcher has a very specialized content focus, as the Invisible Web yields more comprehensive results than searchers receive with search engines on the Visible Web.
2. In order to use a specialized search interface, as these specialized search interfaces give a high level of control over search engine input and output.
3. Using the Invisible Web gives a level of precision and recall that is not available with search engines such as Google.
4. The Invisible Web has a significantly higher level of authority than the Visible Web.
5. The material found in the Invisible Web is probably not available anywhere else on the Web (Sherman and Price, 2007, p. 92).

Thus, we have defined why to use the Invisible Web. Similarly, there are five reasons that describe when it is appropriate to use the Invisible Web.

1. When the searcher is familiar with the subject. This is particularly true when the subject has a specialized jargon or vocabulary.
2. When the searcher is an experienced researcher and has extensive experience with specific research tools and research techniques.
3. When the searcher wants or needs a precise answer, not a list of general resources such as are often in result lists from general search engines.
4. When the searcher desires authoritative, exhaustive results.
5. When the searcher wants the most timely results possible (Sherman and Price, 2007, p. 93).

Chris Sherman and Gary Price, in their seminal book, *The Invisible Web: Uncovering Information Sources Search Engines Can't See*, include a list of the best Invisible Web categories. I have included this list here because, while some changes could be made, it cannot be improved upon. It is comprehensive and for a more detailed description of each category, the reader is encouraged to consult their book.

1. Public Company Filings
2. Telephone Numbers
3. Custom Maps and Driving Directions
4. Results of Clinical Trials
5. Patent Information

   6. Out-of-Print Books
   7. Library Catalogs
   8. Authoritative and Specialized Databases
   9. Environmental Information
10. Historical Stock Quotes
11. Historical Documents and Images
12. Company Directories
13. Searchable Subject Bibliographies
14. Economic Information
15. Award Winners
16. Job Postings
17. Philanthropy and Grant Information
18. Translation Tools
19. Postal Codes
20. Basic Demographic Information
21. Interactive School Finders
22. Campaign Financing Information
23. Weather Data
24. Product Catalogs
25. Art Gallery Holdings (Sherman and Price, 2007, pp. 96–103)

The first three chapters of this book discuss what is in the Invisible Web, why it performs better than standard search engines in searching the Visible Web, and when it can be of value to searchers. Before going forward to a series of categories that describe "good" Invisible Web sites, let's enumerate what is not on either the Visible or Invisible Web.

1. Proprietary database and information services.
2. Most government and public records.
3. Scholarly journals or other valuable information.
4. Full text magazines and newspapers (Sherman and Price, 2007, p. 104).

4

Art and Architecture

Much of the material on the Internet and the World Wide Web deals with art and architecture. The materials that are found there can be of great value to librarians and their patrons only if they can access them. These areas are problems for search engines because so many of them include large numbers of images and, as mentioned earlier, images are typically not found using general purpose search engines. Furthermore, most of the major art museums that offer images for the Web user provide access to them through their database so they will not be found in result lists returned by standard search engines. As with all resource chapters in this book, the description of the Web site uses the site's own words wherever possible. If someone not on the museum staff were to try to describe them, there would be far too many "great site" and "wonderful information" comments to be of any value to the school librarian. In using the site information as a guide, you will find information on the artists in the database, perhaps the address of the museum, and even some history of the art collection.

Chapter 4, Art and Architecture is divided into two sections. The first section is about Art Resources and the second section is about Architecture Resources.

ART

The Guggenheim

http://www.guggenheim.org/

The name, Guggenheim, is recognized by many in the public. It is "an internationally renowned art museum and one of the most significant architectural icons of the 20th century. . . . the Guggenheim Museum is at once a vital cultural center, an educational institution, and the heart of an international network of museums." Visitors are offered special exhibitions of modern and contemporary art as well as lectures by artists and critics. One can attend performances and film screenings or sign up for art classes for teens and adults. Daily tours are led by experienced docents. While the Guggenheim was founded based on a collection of early modern masterpieces, today it offers an expanding collection of art from the twentieth century to today. The Guggenheim site has a search engine that allows the user to search by artist and by work. There are also links to the Guggenheim's museums in Venice, Bilbao, Berlin, and Abu Dhabi.

LouvreMuseum Official Website

http://www.louvre.fr/llv/commun/home.jsp?bmLocale=en

The Louvre is located in the heart of Paris, France. "Beginning in 2005, developments delivered:

- more thematic trails and in-depth studies, building a rich collection of multi-media and cultural resources
- more languages, extending the museum's reach to an even wider global public
- a personalized online space for individual visitors
- a dedicated children's space for younger visitors
- specialist research resources (scholarly publications and databases online)
- mobile tools for use in the museum itself
- online ticket sales for faster access to the collections."

Current, past, and future exhibitions are listed on the museum's Web site, with complete digitized images from the exhibitions and detailed descriptions of the work shown and information about the artist. The site can also be of value to foreign language students as it is available in both English and French.

National Gallery of Art, Washington, DC

http://www.nga.gov/

One of many museums located in Washington D.C., the Web site of the National Gallery of Art has several available search tools. Many images of items and the collection may be searched by artist, title, or subject. Numerous online tours are contained in the site that will assist teachers and librarians in curriculum planning as well as patrons who are preparing for a visit to the National Gallery of Art when they are in Washington.

Smithsonian American Art Museum and the Renwick Gallery

http://americanart.si.edu/

"The Smithsonian American Art Museum, the nation's first collection of American art, is an unparalleled record of the American experience. The collection captures the aspirations, character and imagination of the American people throughout three centuries. The American Art Museum is the home to one of the largest and most inclusive collections of American art in the world. Its artworks reveal key aspects of America's rich artistic and cultural history from the colonial period to today." Among the works of 7,000 artists in this collection, you will find those of the well-known John Singleton Copley, Gilbert Stuart, Winslow Homer, and John Singer Sargent. The works of well-known female artists include those of Mary Cassatt, Georgia O'Keeffe, and Helen Frankenthaler. The Search Collections link on the Smithsonian's Web site is vital to find exactly what you are looking for in its extensive collection. It is so complete and has so many striking images that the art teacher and the librarian will find it of great value. This is probably my favorite American art Web site. (I mentioned that I would not say how much I liked Web sites, but this is so visually striking I could not resist!)

Artcyclopedia: The Fine Art Search Engine

http://www.artcyclopedia.com/

"Artcyclopedia is a form of Internet search engine. The main mode of searching within the site, and the main way that web surfers find their way to us, is a search on an artist's name. Therefore, this is what we generally look for:

- sufficient information spread around the Internet for us to add value. In the most extreme case, if the only high-quality information about an artist is at his or her own website, then web surfers are better served by just staying on Google.
- the artist's name and the searcher must have sufficient awareness of the exact name. If nobody is searching for the artist, then nobody will end up at the artist page anyway. The existence of a page on Artcyclopedia will do little if anything to promote the artist.
- "museum-quality art." However we have no desire to be gatekeepers, i.e. arbiters of quality and merit, so we normally take our cue from museum curators worldwide. If they are collecting and showing an artist's work, that's a signal to us that the artist has significance."

This site has links to more than 80,000 art works by more than 8,000 artists. The search form is contained on the main page. The most popular artists searched for in the last month uses a different browsing tool.

Collage

http://collage.cityoflondon.gov.uk/collage/app

The City of London Library & Art Gallery Electronic (COLLAGE) has a surprise here. COLLAGE does not represent a form of art, but rather is the acronym for City of London Library & Art Gallery Electronic. COLLAGE "is a computerized information system providing quick and easy access to large areas of Guildhall's wonderful visual collections. It invites you to explore the collections using a range of enquiry points. You can then view high quality images of the works on screen, read information about them, and order color prints and digital files." More than 20,000 works from the Guildhall in London are digitized for the site.

The Getty: The Getty Research Institute

http://www.getty.edu/index.html

The Getty Museums are located in greater Los Angeles, California. A part of the GettyMuseum site, this Website includes the Library catalog searching across multiple databases, collection inventories and finding aids, research guides and bibliographies, digital collections, article and research databases, collecting and provenance research, and the Photo Study collection. The search feature is at the top of the main page and allows the user to search the entire site. This is one of the most user-friendly search features.

Kyoto National Museums Online Database

http://www.kyohaku.go.jp/eng/syuzou/index.html

"An image database of the Kyoto National Museums database. Search the collections of the Kyoto National Museum by keyword or category to view comprehensive images of objects that interest you. This database currently contains over 10,000 images of over 5,000 objects or sets of objects from the museum collection." This Web site is limited to Japanese artists and works, but is a gold mine for those interested in Asian art. The images contained on the site are stunning.

Smithsonian National Portrait Gallery

http://www.npg.si.edu/

"The Smithsonian's National Portrait Gallery tells the history of America through individuals who have shaped its culture. Through the visual arts, performing arts and new media, the Portrait Gallery portrays poets and presidents, visionaries and villains, actors and activists whose lives tell the American story." The site has broad appeal not only for art teachers, but also for social studies teachers who want to try a different approach in teaching of U.S. history. Students preparing research studies can find images to allow their readers to see what a person looked like and how they were dressed.

Metropolitan Museum of Art, New York

http://www.metmuseum.org/

"The Metropolitan Museum of Art is one of the world's largest and finest art museums. Its collections include more than two million works of art spanning five thousand years of world culture, from prehistory to the present and from every part of the globe." MOMA was founded in 1870, and it is located in New York City's Central Park. Visitors to MOMA reach close to 5,000,000 each year. This is one of the most complete art sites available, either on the Visible or Invisible Web with nearly 400,000 works of art in many mediums that have been digitized.

National Gallery, London

http://www.nationalgallery.org.uk/

"The collection spans the period from 1260 until 1900 and is made up of Western European paintings. The collection of 20th century art is held at the Tate Modern. Several search modes are available." A strong search engine is available that allows users to search by artist's name, by the number of the work, or by the gallery number.

State Hermitage Museum Digital Collection

http://www.hermitagemuseum.org/fcgi-bin/db2www/browse.mac/category ?selLang=English

"Find artwork by selecting colors from a palette or by sketching shapes on a canvas. Or, refine existing search results by requesting all artwork with comparable visual attributes." Advanced search technologies are available and allow users to search by a large number of search criteria.

V&A Images: The Victoria and Albert Museum

http://www.vandaimages.com/

"V&A Images is the versatile picture agency of the V&A with an ever-expanding collection including the Theatre Collections, Museum of Childhood and the National Art Library. Our images are supplied to professional and commercial image buyers worldwide." When its "pioneering" photographic studio was built in 1858, it was created to record the construction of the building and its acquisitions and this first collection of photos is considered the best nineteenth-century visual documentation of a major building; "as the image collection grew, the need arose for a picture library, in its current form it is now known as V&A Images." A free registration feature allows users some advanced features that regular browsers would not be able to access. Please note the strong copyright notice so users must beware of the use of the images found on this Web site.

Van Gogh Museum

http://www.vangoghmuseum.nl/vgm/index.jsp?page=425&lang=en

A visitor must travel to the Netherlands to see the actual Museum. "The Van Gogh Museum contains the largest collection of paintings by Vincent van Gogh in the world. It provides the opportunity to keep track of the artist's developments, or compare his paintings to works by other artists from the 19th century in the collection. The museum also holds an extensive offer of exhibitions on various subjects from 19th-century art history." Van Gogh is a popular artist in art history classes and this is a great site to accompany lectures and assignments about him for students.

Axis: The Online Resource for Contemporary Art

http://www.axisweb.org/

"Axis is the best online resource for information about contemporary art. The website features profiles of professional artists and curators, interviews, discussions, art news, debates and showcases the artists to watch." Students can use the constantly expanding directory of more than 2,500 profiles of artists and curators. This Web site offers audio, video, biographies, and even an events listing. Those artworks selected for this directory reflect both the high quality and diversity in the art being produced today. A few disclaimers: first, the scope is limited to the United Kingdom, and second, it deals exclusively with contemporary art.

ARCHITECTURE

Cities and Building Database

http://content.lib.washington.edu/buildingsweb/index.html

"The Cities and Buildings Database is a collection of digitized images of buildings and cities drawn from across time and throughout the world, available to students, researchers and educators on the web." When this database was begun in 1995, it was to provide a multi-disciplinary resource for students, faculty, and others in academia. Since then, it holds a steadily growing research with "contributions from a wide range of scholars, and contains images ranging from New York to Central Asia, from African villages, to the Parc de la Villette, and conceptual sketches and models of Frank Gehry's Experience Music Project." Because these images were scanned from original slides or have been pulled from documents in the public domain, students and teachers with access to the Web can use them freely in the classroom. This would be helpful for students who need to illustrate their research projects.

Council on Tall Buildings and Urban Habitat (CTBUH)

http://www.ctbuh.org/

"Founded in 1969, the Council's mission is to disseminate multi-disciplinary information on tall buildings and sustainable urban environments, to maximize the international interaction of professionals involved in creating the built environment, and to make the latest knowledge available to professionals in a useful form." An international not-for-profit organization, the Council is funded by architecture, engineering, planning, development, and construction professionals and has become the recognized source of information on tall buildings internationally. As countries vie for "The World's Tallest Building," CTBUH is in charge of the criteria upon which height is measured. The Council's journal is available for purchase and might be a consideration for libraries in institutions with strong art programs.

Archinform Index of Persons

http://eng.archinform.net/archli/index.htm

"This database for international architecture, originally emerging from records of interesting building projects from architecture students, has meanwhile become the largest online-database about worldwide architects and buildings from past to present." Included in this database, students will find over 29,000, mostly twentieth-century building projects, both built and planned from architects and planners. The database can be searched by architect, town, or keyword. The indices use a query form. For most of the entries, teachers and students will find the name, address, keywords, and information about further literature. "Some entries include images, comments, links to other Websites or internal links." Again, this database delivers more that the title would imply. This is a valuable resource for several areas in a technology curriculum.

SPIRO Architecture Slides Library

http://www.mip.berkeley.edu/spiro/

Named in honor of a late architectural historian, Professor Emeritus Spiro Kostof, this acronym stands for Slide and Photography Image Retrieval Online (SPIRO). "SPIRO is the visual online public access catalog to the 35mm slide collection of the Architecture Visual Resources Library (AVRL) at the University of California at Berkeley." This collection includes more than 250,000 slides and 20,000 photographs. "SPIRO permits access to the collection by seven access points which may be used independently or in combination:

- historical period;
- place;
- personal name;
- object name;
- subject terms;
- source of image;
- image identification number."

5

Magazine Articles and Books

The Internet material contained in this chapter about magazine articles and books is, for the most part, free. However, some of the Web sites require a registration and some of them have a portion that is free and a portion that is fee-based. At the present time, most of the full text magazine articles your users can find on the Web are either part of subscription databases or are not available. The book resources detailed in this chapter are, almost exclusively, books that are out of copyright and freely available. It remains to be seen what effect projects such as Google Books will have on this availability. As with all resource chapters in the book, the description of the Web site uses the site's own words wherever possible. If I were to use my words, there would be far too many "great site" and "wonderful information" comments to be of any value to the school librarian. This chapter is divided into two sections, the first presents magazine articles, and the second presents book resources.

MAGAZINE ARTICLES

Directory of Open Access Journals

http://www.doaj.org/

"The Directory of Open Access Journals covers free, full text, quality controlled scientific and scholarly journals. We aim to cover all subjects and languages. There are now 5938 journals in the directory. Currently 2,495 journals are searchable at article level. As of today 491,520 articles are included in the DOAJ service." While this has wide coverage, it does not include journals from most major professional organizations.

Find Articles at BNet

http://findarticles.com/

"The hub of the CBS Interactive Business Network, BNET.com provides working professionals with the advice and insights they need to get ahead in today's workplace. It isn't a site for those who merely punch the clock: It's for business leaders—of today and the future—who believe in the meaning of work and who know that nurturing excellence in their staff and their organization is the true measure of success." The Web site requires a subscription to some of the publications in order to get full-text magazine articles.

HighWire: Stanford University

http://highwire.stanford.edu/

"HighWire provides online hosting and technology solutions to publishers, management tools for librarians and unique search functionality for researchers." They have recently updated their portal and are asking for comments. Their portal offers the following features for librarians:

- Easy to use online administration of cross-publication accounts and IP address
- One stop COUNTER3-compliant usage reports, as well as detailed use info on specific sections
- Full-text search and browse, as well as valuable tools to refine search results, such as KeyWord in Context, CiteMap, MatchMaker and Topic Map applications
- Alerts on issues, topics, authors, new publications, changes to subscriptions at your request
- General information such as publication frequency, free back issue policies, ppv lists and more
- Downloadable A to Z lists of all publications hosted by HighWire."

While there is an inference that not all of the publications are available in full-text, I did not find that to be the case.

MagPortal

http://www.magportal.com/

"MagPortal.com® is a search engine and directory for finding online magazine articles." It also provides feeds for use on other websites. The site was officially launched on March 28, 2000."

"MagPortal.com is owned and operated by Hot Neuron LLC, a company that specializes in applying novel research and ideas to software and internet services development. This site makes use of the Hot Neuron SimilarityTM software package to measure the similarity between articles." There are no big name magazines here, but the articles can round out an exhaustive search.

BOOKS

New York Times Books

http://www.nytimes.com/pages/books/

On this Web site, there are full-text book reviews available back to 1981. Several different modes of search are available. A log-in is no longer required to access the reviews and much other information about books and authors. This will be of particular value to English teachers who want their students to read reviews of the books chosen for book reports.

Google Books

http://books.google.com/

"Book Search works just like web search. Try a search on Google Books or on Google.com. When we find a book with content that contains a match for your search terms, we'll link to it in your search results. If the book is out of copyright, or the publisher has given us permission, you'll be able to see a preview of the book, and in some cases, the entire text. If it's in the public domain, you're free to download a PDF copy." This site has caused much controversy in the world of book publishing because it seemed to be a run around ownership of the book's content. The concept can be valuable for librarians, but the execution leaves many things open to copyright interpretation.

Bibliomania

http://www.bibliomania.com/

"Free online literature with more than 2000 Classic Texts. Literature book notes, Author biographies, book summaries and reference books. Read classic fiction, drama, poetry, short stories and contemporary articles and interviews. Study guides to the most read books and Help for Teachers." The study guides are the most help to users because the study guides enhance the readers' understanding of works that are often complex.. The books themselves appear in most out-of-copyright Web sites.

Free eBooks by Project Gutenberg

http://www.gutenberg.org/wiki/Main_Page

"Project Gutenberg is the place where you can download over 33,000 free ebooks to read on your PC, iPad, Kindle, Sony Reader, or iPhone, Android or other portable device. We carry high quality ebooks: Our ebooks were previously published by bona fide publishers and digitized by us with the help of thousands of volunteers. All our ebooks can be freely downloaded: Choose between ePub, Kindle, HTML and simple text formats. No fee or registration is required." This site has been hosted by several academic institutions. Eventually, I believe that these works will all be available in e-book form.

6

Business and Economics

The amount of business and economics data has exploded over the past few years going from material that only fell in proprietary services such as Orbit and Dialog to the vast amount of data that is available on the Web today. While much of this business and economic data is on the Visible Web and can be accessed by standard search engines such as Google or Yahoo, that data and material is often outdated as soon as it is posted and available. The Invisible Web is the key here as the search process in various databases can provide material that is current within seconds. It is literally the most current information on business and economics available on the Web. Again, as with all resource chapters in the book, the description of the Web site uses the site's own words wherever possible.

Commerce Business Daily

http://www.cbd-net.com/

"Search the notices in the FedBizOpps (FBO), formerly the Commerce Business Daily (CBD), for federal procurement bidding opportunities, contracts awarded, special notices and surplus government sales. You can search using keywords or phrases relevant to your business or select from over 100 business categories using NEPAC's FBO Online search engine service." This site has limited applicability for school libraries, but is very useful for public and academic librarians and their patrons. This reflects the level of sophistication in the material, a level that would be largely wasted on K-12 students.

Economic Indicators Main Page

http://www.gpo.gov/fdsys/browse/collection.action?collectionCode=ECONI

The Economic Indicators Main Page, a monthly publication, has been available since 1995. Prepared by the Council of Economic Advisers for the Joint Economic Committee, this Web site "provides economic information on gross domestic product, income, employment, production, business activity, prices, money, credit, security markets, Federal finance, and international statistics." If you need economic indicators back to 1948, you will need to search the Federal Reserve Archival System for Economic Research (FRASER) (http://fraser.stlouisfed.org/). This information is provided through a partnership between the Government Printing Office (GPO) and the Federal Reserve Bank of St. Louis. However, users need to know that FRASER is not an "official" version of economic indicators and "GPO cannot guarantee the authenticity or completeness of the data." This site will assist business and social studies teachers, along with librarians and patrons, by providing both current and historical examinations of the leading economic indicators.

GuideStar

http://www2.guidestar.org/

"The mission of GuideStar is to revolutionize philanthropy by providing information that advances transparency, enables users to make better decisions, and encourages charitable giving. GuideStar gathers and publicizes information about nonprofit organizations. Their reach is far and wide. The database is broad and deep." GuideStar encourages nonprofits to share their information fully. Nonprofits are able to post on GuidStar at no cost and GuideStar would like them to post their mission, programs, leaders, goals, accomplishments. Reports from these nonprofits can be updated regularly. GuideStar then combines this information from the nonprofits with other data they have obtained from many other sources. As budgets decline and everyone is seeking outside funding, this database may be helpful to begin searching for places to submit proposals for projects. As school budgets become tighter, it is incumbent on users to search for non-traditional funding sources and this Web site can help.

Hoover's Business Information

http://www.hoovers.com/

"Hoover's Inc., a D&B Company, puts you on the fastest path to business. They deliver comprehensive insight and analysis about the companies, industries and people that drive the economy, along with the powerful tools to find and connect to the right people to get business done." This database offers proprietary business information through several sources including the Internet, data feeds, and wireless devices. Hoover's also has agreements with other online services. A subscription fee may be required for some in-depth information. This Web site is considered the old standby for business and economics teachers. However, it is not particularly intuitive and has almost more information than students can handle, but it is useful. It will be up to the librarian to help teachers and students understand the information available here.

Kompass Worldwide Company Search Engine

http://us.kompass.com/

"The Kompass classification containing over 57,000 Kompass Classification Codes has been developed over the past 60 years. Recently revised, it is now standardized worldwide and provides users with an unparalleled ability to search the extensive worldwide database." This database is indexed in 26 languages which allow users to find products and services in their own native languages and might allows your foreign language teachers to ask students to seek products in the language they are studying. This classification has a seven digit code with the first two digits "representing the industrial group, the next three the product or service group and the final two identify the product or service." A warning: the complete data is only available by subscription, and the amount of free data is limited.

Morningstar Document Research

http://www.tenkwizard.com/

"Morningstar® Document Research streamlines public company research by providing navigation tools to help quickly extract the most important pieces of information from these documents." A fee is required to gain access to the information. This is a site that should be considered where funds are available or demand for the data is high.

PricewaterhouseCoopers Money Tree Report

https://www.pwcmoneytree.com/MTPublic/ns/index.jsp

The MoneyTree Report is "a quarterly study of venture capital investment activity in the United States. As a collaboration between PricewaterhouseCoopers and the National Venture Capital Association based upon data from Thomson Reuters, it is the only industry-endorsed research of its kind." The MoneyTree Report offers aggregate trend data beginning in 1995 and information on emerging companies that receive financing as well as those venture capital firms financing these emerging companies. This database is used heavily by the financial community and would be useful in the academic community for descriptions of "entrepreneurs, government policymakers and the business press worldwide." The search engine is not particularly easy to use and much of the information has been made available by the *San Jose Mercury News*.

ThomasNet.com

http://www.thomasnet.com/

"Search ThomasNet to find manufacturers, distributors and service providers—from Actuators to Zirconium and everything in between." This database provides detailed information about businesses. It was formerly known as the Thomas Register.

Filings and Forms from the U.S. Securities and Exchange Commission

http://www.sec.gov/edgar.shtml

"All companies, foreign and domestic, are required to file registration statements, periodic reports, and other forms electronically through EDGAR. Anyone can access and download this information for free. Here you'll find links to a complete list of filings available through EDGAR and instructions for searching the EDGAR database." It is a very specialized Web site and will be more appropriate for large public and academic libraries than for school libraries. However, if your K–12 teachers have a stock club, members may be also interested in this database.

Better Business Bureau

http://www.bbb.org/us/

This Web site allows interested people to access Better Business Bureau reports through their individual offices. Because it is a slow loading site, you must be sure your Internet connection is robust enough for multiple users. Once your public library users discover this site, they may be checking for legitimate companies whose advertisements they read in the local newspaper or in advertisements they receive through the mail.

Dow Jones Historical Stock Market Prices

http://finance.yahoo.com/q/hp?s=%5EDJI

This Webs site allows searchers to see Dow Jones High, Open, Close, Low, and Volume for stocks since October 1, 1928. The reports can be daily, weekly, or monthly. This is specific for the historical process, but much other business information is available on the Dow Jones homepage.

Historical Quotes

http://bigcharts.marketwatch.com/historical/

"This Historical Quotes tool allows you to look up a security's exact closing price. Type in the symbol and a historical date to view a quote and mini chart for that security." This database is very similar to the Dow Jones site noted above, but it lacks the additional business information contained on that site.

Calculating Stocks' Value from the Dismal Scientist

http://www.economy.com/dismal/blog/blog.asp?cid=123340

According to the database creators, a market calculator does not provide hot buying tips or an early sell signal, but it is a useful way to treat equity prices as an economic indicator. "At their most efficient, markets aggregate the opinions of millions of investors, opinions that can influence business investment, consumer spending and ultimately the path of overall economic growth. The calculator's model draws together fundamental drivers of equity value—earnings growth, interest rates and commodity prices—to produce a view of 'fair value.'" Moody's Economy.com's forecast assumptions are shown on the chart, and it allows readers to add their own assumptions as well. Many high schools have projects where students have a certain amount of funds and have to invest them and this site will assist in this type of project.

Economagic.com: Economic Time Series Page

http://www.economagic.com/

"This page is meant to be a comprehensive site of free, easily available economic time series data useful for economic research, in particular economic forecasting. This site (set of web pages) was started in 1996 to help students in an Applied Forecasting class. The idea was to give students easy access to large amounts of data, and to be able to quickly get charts of that data." Teachers will find this information during class by using the computer and overhead projector to retrieve series and quickly do manipulations. Currently, the database has more than 200,000 time series for which data and custom charts can be retrieved and modified. It also has Excel files for all time series available. Most of the data is from the United States, with the bulk of the employment data by local area—state, county, Metropolitan Statistical Area, cities and towns. Teachers of economics and librarians whose collections may be limited will find this a helpful site.

FDIC Regional Economic Conditions

http://www2.fdic.gov/recon/

In the beginning, Regional Economic Conditions (RECON) was designed to help the FDIC in the examination process by providing economic information at local areas: state, MSA (Metropolitan Statistical Area), and county levels. It is helpful in the analysis of risks facing financial institutions. Easy access to timely, high-quality information about economic conditions and risks might be beneficial to teachers, students, and the general public. RECON provides access to anyone with the Internet access to find this information and "to view standard graphs, tables, and maps depicting economic conditions and how they have changed over time. RECON contains a 'shopping cart' feature that allows the user to assemble charts and tables of interest and then print them together at the end of their session." The FDIC has taken a lot of criticism recently but not because of this Web site. This site contains much valuable economic and business information that teachers and librarians alike will find valuable, because of the emphasis on local economic data and information.

Free Economic, Demographic, and Financial Data

http://www.economy.com/freelunch/default.asp

"Freelunch.com is a free service provided by Moody's Economy.com, a leading independent provider of economic, financial, country, and industry research that helps businesses, governments, and professional investors worldwide meet their diverse planning and information needs." These databases offer more than 165 million economic, financial, and demographic time series covering more than 180 countries and their sub-regions. Because this is one of Moody's Economy.com economic databases, it is guaranteed to be accurate and timely. The emergence of global economies makes this a site of value, particularly in international business classes.

Penn World Table, Center for International Comparisons at the University of Pennsylvania

http://pwt.econ.upenn.edu/

Detailed information here at this Web site is found in eight different areas of research interest. This site is difficult to use and an advanced knowledge of economics is required making it most useful in an academic library.

Salary.com

http://www.salary.com/salary/index.asp

"Enter your job and geographic location and Salary.com will tell you how much you should be earning. . . .Salary.com is now part of Kenexa. Kenexa® provides business solutions for human resources. We help global organizations multiply business success by identifying the best individuals for every job and fostering optimal work environments for every organization." This is a Web site that students getting ready to choose an occupation will find useful because it gives them information about salaries that they may eventually earn.

United States Bureau of Labor Statistics (BLS)

http://www.bls.gov/

"The Bureau of Labor Statistics of the U.S. Department of Labor is the principal Federal agency responsible for measuring labor market activity, working conditions, and price changes in the economy." The mission of BLS is "to collect, analyze, and disseminate essential economic information to support public and private decision-making." BLS is an independent statistical agency that serves "diverse user communities by providing products and services that are objective, timely, accurate, and relevant."

USAJobs: Working for America

http://www.usajobs.gov/

"This is a United States Office of Personnel Management website. USAJOBS is the Federal Government's official one-stop source for Federal jobs and employment information." The database has a strong emphasis on veterans, individuals with disabilities, and recent graduates searching for jobs. It would be helpful for these and other job seekers in any type of library.

FlipDog

http://www.flipdog.com/

"FlipDog is a great place to find jobs and advance your career. Whether you're looking for a new job or researching employment opportunities, FlipDog allows you to quickly search and find the information you need most. And since FlipDog is powered by Monster, you'll have access to the largest database of jobs and the most helpful career development tools." This is yet another Web site that will be useful in public libraries where people request information on job possibilities.

O*Net OnLine

http://online.onetcenter.org/

"The O*NET program is the nation's primary source of occupational information. Central to the project is the O*NET database, containing information on hundreds of standardized and occupation-specific descriptors." This database is free to the public. It is continually updated through surveys sent to a broad range of workers from each occupation. O*NET OnLine, an interactive application for exploring and searching occupations, is the basis of this company's Career Exploration Tools, which are "a set of valuable assessment instruments for workers and students looking to find or change careers." It is a better Web site than the Occupational Outlook Handbook Web site because it is updated more frequently and is based on worker input.

7

Education

No chapter in this book has as much information that can be of value to the school librarian or education students in an academic setting than this chapter about education materials. Not only are there a great many sites on the Web about education, we will also see that in Chapter 8, Gateways, many of these sites are only accessible through the Invisible Web. The Web sites presented in the chapter are not just for teachers; they can profitably be shared with students as they seek the best and most up-to-date education materials. As with all resource chapters in this book, the description of the Web site uses the site's own words wherever possible.

Current Awareness Program: The Landmark P

http://landmark-project.com/ca/

This Web site could also be a part of Chapter 5, Magazine Articles and Books, because Current Awareness is a monthly bibliography with the most recent educational literature from a large number of journals. Provided by the Division of Instructional Technology in North Carolina's Department of Public Instruction in partnership with The Landmark Project, this group has identified over 200 education- and technology-related topics of interest to educators. On a monthly basis, staff from the North Carolina's Information Center reviews newly arrived journals and other materials. They then match articles with education and technology topics which are given links to short citations for the articles. This linkage provides educators with easy searches for information on their topic of interest. Unfortunately, no indication is given of when this Web site has been updated which sometimes leads to user frustration.

Distance Education Learning Technologies

http://node.on.ca/

Visitors to this Web site are typically looking for programs or materials that pertain to distance education. The materials and information available is useful for students or teachers and offers the best materials gathered in one location. This site has become much more important to educators in K–12 schools because of the proliferation of cyber schools.

Education Finance Statistics Center

http://nces.ed.gov/edfin/

Sponsored by the Institute of Education Sciences of the U.S. Department of Education, this Web site offers financial information pertaining to public elementary/secondary education. The finance graphs offer summary figures and tables. If your users need information specific to public school district finance data or comparisons with other school districts, this and school district fiscal and non-fiscal data over time is provided on the Data Tools page. The data tools are a powerful part of the page, but they do not always "play well" with Microsoft Excel. This information may be useful when comparing student achievement scores from district to district. (It is no surprise to learn that students in the highly funded school districts usually have much higher achievement scores than those in poorly funded districts.)

The Gateway to 21st Century Skills: National Education Association

http://www.thegateway.org/

This Web site could also be considered a "gateway site" because it is a consortium effort. NEA provides educators with quick and easy access to thousands of educational resources found on various federal, state, university, and non-profit as well as commercial Internet sites. This site contains a wide variety of educational resource types including activities, lesson plans, online projects, and assessment items designed for classroom use.

Any organization or individual who wants to have records for their resources on this site must join the Gateway Consortium which assures quality in the content. An application and review process, done at the collection level rather than the individual level, means that each collection is evaluated for authoritativeness, quality, and availability based on criteria developed and adopted by the Gateway Consortium. If teachers want to review the criteria, it can be located in the Gateway Consortium Governance document. Some would disregard this site because its "owner" is the NEA, but you have to overlook the sponsorship as it has a wealth of good educational material.

National Center for Educational Statistics

http://nces.ed.gov/

"The National Center for Education Statistics fulfills a Congressional mandate to collect, collate, analyze, and report complete statistics on the condition of American education; conduct and publish reports; and review and report on education activities internationally." This Web site may be of more use to administrators than teachers, but it is still the first place to go for comparative educational statistics. It may be also very useful for teachers in K–12 schools or faculty members in higher education who are preparing a proposal for funding.

PBS Teachers' Resources for the Classroom

http://www.pbs.org/teachers

"PBS Teachers is PBS' national web destination for high-quality pre-K–12 educational resources. Here you'll find classroom materials suitable for a wide range of subjects and grade levels. We provide thousands of lesson plans, teaching activities, on-demand video assets, and interactive games and simulations." All resources are correlated to state and national educational standards and they are linked to PBS award-winning on-air and online programming such as *NOVA*, *Nature*, *Cyberchase*, and *Between the Lions*. Certainly in the coming years there will also be a correlation to the Core Standards.

Search for Public Schools

http://nces.ed.gov/ccd/schoolsearch/

This Web site allows teachers, librarians, and others to find public schools across the country. You can search within the site by school name, school address, or state.

The Educator's Reference Desk

http://www.eduref.org/

The Educator's Reference Desk site has been built from 25 years of experience providing high-quality resources and services to educators. I like the Question Archives because almost any question I think of has already been addressed. "From the Information Institute of Syracuse, the people who created

AskERIC, the Gateway to Educational Materials, and the Virtual Reference Desk, the Educator's Reference Desk brings you the resources you have come to depend on. 2,000+ lesson plans, 3,000+ links to online education information, and 200+ question archive responses."

Ericae.net

http://ericae.net/

"With the explosive growth of the Internet and the resultant increased use of information, ERIC, as a system, is now widely recognized as the central source in the education and social science fields." The professional staff is small at ERIC, and it has contracted abstractors at the Cygnus Corporation. They and several student assistants have worked to make ERIC/AE viewed as "the central source for assessment and evaluation information." This staff has forged numerous partnerships for the electronic dissemination of information and has created active Web pages as well as having established an active listserv; the staff participates in several others. The staff has also created pathfinders to help users locate information within their scope, created both an on-line journal and an extensive full-text library. They also provide workshops on assessment and Internet resources. There are, however, some currency issues with the site.

College Navigator

http://nces.ed.gov/collegenavigator/

- "Begin your Search from the search menu or choose http://nces.ed.gov/collegenavigator/
- Refine your search by selecting More Search Options to use additional search criteria.
- Build a list of schools using My Favorites for side-by-side comparisons.
- Pinpoint school locations with an interactive map.
- Export search results into a spreadsheet.
- Save your session including search options, results, and favorites."

This is another site that belongs under the broad umbrella of the National Center for Educational Statistics.

Peterson's Graduate Schools

http://www.petersons.com/graduate-schools.aspx

"Now is the time when many students are beginning to think about grad school, and that means it's important to start the thought process by looking at information for finding the right graduate school." This will be especially helpful for the academic librarian in an institution with undergraduate students who may think that continuing their education is preferable to entering the job market.

Scholarship Search

http://apps.collegeboard.com/cbsearch_ss/welcome.jsp

"We created this online tool to help you locate scholarships, internships, grants, and loans that match your education level, talents, and background. Complete the brief questionnaire and Scholarship Search will find potential opportunities from our database of more than 2,300 sources of college funding, totaling nearly $3 BILLION in available aid!" Librarians must remind their students that the more accurate information they enter on this Web site, the better the chance that the Web site will be able to match them to financial aid sources. Therefore, they must complete all the sections of the online questionnaire for the best results.

Scholarships.com

http://www.scholarships.com/

"As a leading scholarship search service financial aid information resource, Scholarships.com plays a primary role in helping students make the decisions that shape their lives. On Scholarships.com, students are connected with tools to aid in researching and finding financial aid for college, as well as choosing a campus that's right for them." The creators of this Web site regularly update the information which allows students to search 2.7 million college scholarships and grants worth over $19 billion and quickly arrive at a list of awards for which they qualify. What is remarkable here is that all this information is free to the student. I cannot say that this site is any better than Scholarship Search. Guidance counselors, librarians, and students will probably want to use both Web sites and compare the results.

Academic Info

http://www.academicinfo.net/

This database was founded by Mike Madin, a librarian, in 1998 and at the present time is maintained by many contributors. "AcademicInfo is an online education resource center with extensive subject guides, a plethora of online degrees, online courses and distance learning information from a selection of online accredited schools. Our mission is to provide free, independent and accurate information and resources for prospective and current students (and other researchers)." This database features over 25,000+ hand-picked resources and the Web site is updated a daily basis. However, this site would benefit from a more comprehensive search tool.

Writer's Complex

http://www.esc.edu/writer

This Web site consists of an assortment of databases related to the college writing processes that are brought together in one place. This is a very helpful site for the writer, but it has some similarity to the Owl sites.

8

Gateways

In a way, this is the most important chapter of resources in the book. While the other chapters consist of specific types of resources and materials, this chapter is about just what is inferred by the title. Each of the described Web sites is a gateway, a portal, or an entrance into the vast array of materials that are on the Invisible Web. Nearly all of these sites cover a wide variety of topics and allow the savvy searcher to mine many different sources for the most in-depth and complete material available on the Web. These sites should be the first place you visit on the Invisible Web unless you are a very experienced searcher and know exactly where you want to begin your search. As with all resource chapters in the book, the descriptions of the Web site use the site's own words wherever possible.

About.com

http://www.about.com/

"With nearly 800 Guides, About.com helps users find solutions to a wide range of daily needs—from parenting, health care and technology to cooking, travel and many others. About.com reaches 40MM average monthly unique visitors in the United States* and 75MM average monthly unique visitors worldwide**." They report that 80 percent of their users arrive at About.com from search engines at a time when they realize that they need something they cannot find. They also work to maintain its relevance to users. "About.com covers more than 70,000 topics, and adds more than 6,000 pieces of new content each week." The site is somewhat slow to load, even with high-speed Internet, and there is no general search on the homepage, so you need to mine further into the site.

AlphaSearch Metasearch Engine

http://www.alphasearch.org/

"On Alphasearch you find a rather extensive on-line encyclopedia with explanations, definitions and meanings for different subjects. About the encyclopedia search you should reach fast to the desired explanations. About the catalogue you can search for one desired word. Our focus at Alphasearch.org is to provide you the possibility to submit your site to an appropriate category inside our directory that really fits to you." There is not a tremendous amount of detail on this Web site, so it should be considered a beginning rather than a destination. One negative point is that the advertising can be overwhelming and is a distraction to the user.

Animal Search

http://www.animalsearch.net/

This huge database allows you to search for information about animals. Searches can be by type, group, geographic area, specific animal, and there is also a miscellaneous search. This should augment information you have in print form and add to information students can find in other databases.

Complete Planet: A Deep Web Directory

http://www.completeplanet.com

According to the creators of this database, "there are hundreds of thousands of databases that contain Deep Web content. CompletePlanet is the front door to these Deep Web databases on the Web and to the thousands of regular search engines." They consider it a first step in trying to find highly topical information. "By tracing through CompletePlanet's subject structure or searching Deep Web sites, you can go to various topic areas, such as energy or agriculture or food or medicine, and find rich content sites not accessible using conventional search engines." CompletePlanet is one of the Web sites that the literature describes as a good starting point for entrance into the Invisible Web.

Internet Archive

http://www.archive.org/

Founded in 1996 and still located in San Francisco, the Internet Archive is a 501(c)(3) non-profit created to build an Internet library. It has a very strong focus on music, audio, and images. "Its purposes include offering permanent access for researchers, historians, scholars, people with disabilities, and the general public to historical collections that exist in digital format." The Archive has been receiving data donations from Alexa Internet and others. By late 1999, the organization started to include more well-rounded collections and now it includes texts, audio, moving images, and software as well as archived Web pages. The Archive "provides specialized services for adaptive reading and information access for the blind and other persons with disabilities."

Intute

http://www.intute.ac.uk/

"Intute is a free online service that helps you to find web resources for your studies and research. With millions of resources available on the Internet, it can be difficult to find useful material." The creators of this Web site "reviewed and evaluated thousands of resources to help you choose key websites in your subject." They also provide The Virtual Training Suite of designed tutorials to help you develop your Internet research skills. These tutorials were written "by lecturers and librarians from universities across the UK." The training piece is valuable for librarians and educators whose students think the only way to get information on the Internet is to Google.

Ipl2: Information You Can Trust

http://www.ipl.org/

"In January 2010, the website ipl2: information you can trust combined the collections of resources from the Internet Public Library (IPL) and the Librarians' Internet Index (LII) websites." Created by thousands of students and volunteers, they continue and maintain the work on the Web site by answering reference questions from an Ask an ipl2 Librarian. "ipl2 is a public service organization and a learning/teaching environment." It has combined two of the best resource collections into one easy-to-use location.

Libdex

http://www.libdex.com/

"Libdex is a worldwide directory of:

- library homepages,
- web-based OPACs,
- Friends of the Library pages, and
- library e-commerce affiliate links.

The directory does not include links to terminal-based OPACs." This site is probably of much more value to public librarians than to school and academic librarians. The topics emphasized on this site, such as Friends of Library pages refer almost exclusively to public libraries.

National Archives

http://www.archives.gov/

"The National Archives and Records Administration (NARA) is the nation's record keeper. Of all documents and materials created in the course of business conducted by the United States Federal government, only 1%-3% are so important for legal or historical reasons that they are kept by us forever." On this governmental Web site, records which are preserved remain available for your use; you can find clues about your family's history, prove a veteran's military service, or look for an historical topic of interest. The magnitude of the National Archives digitization program is truly breathtaking and as it goes forward, this will be the ultimate destination for searches for any kind of government records.

New Zealand Digital Library

http://www.nzdl.org/cgi-bin/library.cgi

"The New Zealand Digital Library project is a research program at The University of Waikato whose aim is to develop the underlying technology for digital libraries and make it available publicly so that others can use it to create their own collections." This Web site provides historical documents, humanitarian and development information, computer science technical reports and bibliographies, literary works, and magazines. These resources are available over the Web through searching and browsing interfaces provided by the Greenstone digital library software.

Resource Shelf

http://www.resourceshelf.com/

This Web site contains "countless high-quality, free resources are available on the web, including databases, lists and rankings, real-time sources, and multimedia." This database is very strongly business-oriented but unfortunately, is not the most intuitive site to try to use.

Smithsonian Institution Libraries and the Smithsonian

http://www.sil.si.edu/ and http://www.si.edu/

"The most comprehensive museum library system in the world, supporting the vital research of the Institution as well as the work of scientists and scholars near and far.... Founded in 1846, the Smithsonian is the world's largest museum and research complex, consisting of 19 museums and galleries, the National Zoological Park and nine research facilities." This is the national museum of the United States and it is a leader in digitization of resources. The search feature is very strong and supports keyword searching. The different museums associated with the Smithsonian make this a destination site in the Invisible Web. Faculty and students at all levels will enjoy finding information here just as they enjoy visiting the Smithsonian when they are in Washington, DC.

Super Searchers Web Page

http://www.infotoday.com/supersearchers/

This page features a growing collection of links to subject-specific Web resources recommended by the world's leading online searchers. "The Super Searchers Web Page is provided as a bonus to readers of the Super Searchers series of books, edited by renowned author and online searcher Reva Basch and published by Information Today, Inc. (CyberAge Books)" Valuable information can be found on the Web site that librarians can use, but other users must beware of the heavy advertising content.

InfoMine

http://infomine.ucr.edu/

"INFOMINE is a virtual library of Internet resources relevant to faculty, students, and research staff at the university level. It contains useful Internet resources such as databases, electronic journals, electronic books, bulletin boards, mailing lists, online library card catalogs, articles, directories of researchers, and many other types of information." INFOMINE was created by librarians from the University of California, Wake Forest University, California State University, the University of Detroit–Mercy as well as other universities and colleges. Because it is a very scholarly site, it is more appropriate for academic or public librarians than for school librarians.

DeepPeep

http://www.deeppeep.org/

"DeepPeep is a search engine specialized in Web forms. The current beta version currently tracks 45,000 forms across 7 domains. DeepPeep helps you discover the entry points to content in Deep Web (aka Hidden Web) sites, including online databases and Web services." The advanced search for this database allows the researcher to perform more specific queries such as specifying keywords or for specific form element labels, i.e., the description of the form attributes. (Forms are a piece of the Invisible Web that cannot be accessed through regular browsers.)

OAIster Database

http://www.oclc.org/oaister/

"OAIster is a union catalog of millions of records representing open access resources that was built by harvesting from open access collections worldwide using the Open Archives Initiative Protocol for Metadata Harvesting (OAI-PMH). Today, OAIster includes more than 25 million records representing digital resources from more than 1,100 contributors." This is OCLC's Invisible Web portal and it has a subscription price for use of this site.

WWW Virtual Library

http://vlib.org/

Tim Berners-Lee created HTML, the Web itself (in 1991 in Geneva) and the WWW Virtual Library (VL). This is the oldest catalog on the Web and, as is "Ipl2: Information You Can Trust." It is managed "by a loose confederation of volunteers, who compile pages of key links for particular areas in which they are expert; even though it isn't the biggest index of the Web, the VL pages are widely recognized as being amongst the highest-quality guides to particular sections of the Web."

9

Government and Consumer Resources

One of the most prolific publishers of information on the World Wide Web is the U.S. government. They have an almost insatiable desire to put "everything" on the Web. The negative concern that goes along with this desire is that much of the information is not available on the Visible Web for two reasons: First, much of the material is in formats that standard Web search engines cannot index and, second, a large amount of the material is available only in databases which are similarly impenetrable to standard search engines. As with all resource chapters in this book, the description of the Web site uses the site's own words wherever possible. This chapter is divided into two sections; the first covers a wide range of government resources and the second section covers consumer resources.

GOVERNMENT RESOURCES

American Fact Finder (US Census Bureau)

http://factfinder.census.gov/home/saff/main.html?_lang=en

A new version of this Web site has just been posted as of the publication of this book. The strong point of the site is the ability to mine almost anything from the census data that has been gathered. You can also refer to the U.S. Census Bureau's main page (http://www.census.gov/). Census data is often used by students to show trends in U.S. history. Patrons in the public library who are seeking census data will be happy to learn about this database.

Congressional Biographical Directory

http://bioguide.congress.gov/biosearch/biosearch.asp

The Web site allows you to locate and read authoritative biographies of all members of the U.S. Congress since 1774. This saves you from researching multiple encyclopedia volumes. It has great potential for U.S. History teachers who wish to compare the backgrounds of members of Congress through the years with their students.

Capitol Hill, the White House and National Politics

http://www.c-span.org/

"C-SPAN is a private, non-profit company, created in 1979 by the cable television industry as a public service. Our mission is to provide public access to the political process. C-SPAN receives no government funding; operations are funded by fees paid by cable and satellite affiliates who carry C-SPAN programming." Every time I visit the C-SPAN site, I find something new and fascinating and the information is very non-partisan.

FedStats

http://www.fedstats.gov/

"FedStats, which has been available to the public since 1997, provides access to the full range of official statistical information produced by the Federal Government without having to know in advance which Federal agency produces which particular statistic. With convenient searching and linking capabilities to more than 100 agencies that provide data and trend information on such topics as economic and population trends, crime, education, health care, aviation safety, energy use, farm production and more, FedStats is your one location for access to the full breadth of Federal statistical information." This is a prime example of a site that traditional browsers will have difficulty using, but it will be very useful if students are matching statistics from one year to the next.

GPO Access Home Page

http://www.gpoaccess.gov/index.html

This site will change during 2011 becoming an archive-only site. "*GPO Access* is a service of the U.S. Government Printing Office that provides free electronic access to a wealth of important information products produced by the Federal Government. The information provided on this site is the official, published version and the information retrieved from *GPO Access* can be used without restriction, unless specifically noted. This free service is funded by the Federal Depository Library Program and has grown out of Public Law 103-40, known as the Government Printing Office Electronic Information Enhancement Act of 1993."

Grants.Gov

http://www.grants.gov/

This is the database to send your users to if they want to find and then apply for federal grants. Many school districts are being forced to look for non-traditional funding sources and this is the best guide I have found for grant-giving agencies. The Web site is managed by the U.S. Department of Health and Human Services and is "an initiative that is having an unparalleled impact on the grant community. Grants.gov was established as a governmental resource named the E-Grants Initiative, part of the President's 2002 Fiscal Year Management Agenda to improve government services to the public. . . . Grants.gov is a central storehouse for information on over 1,000 grant programs and provides access to approximately $500 billion in annual awards." Whether you need to consider preparing a grant proposal or if your school is seeking another source of funds for a special project, this site will be of help.

Historical Census Browser

http://mapserver.lib.virginia.edu/

"The data and terminology presented in the Historical Census Browser are drawn directly from historical volumes of the U.S. Census of Population and Housing. The available data differ somewhat from decade to decade, according to what was collected in the census and the items chosen for transcription to electronic form." The site offers most of the enumerated items from the early decades, but for later decades, only a portion of characteristics have been transcribed. Only states are included with no information below the county level. Western territories were included after statehood, but there is no information for the District of Columbia. Included with the basic counts of population and housing units, all decades contain information on race, gender, and some measure of household size and composition. After 1840, some economic characteristics (education and occupation) are included and in later decades, many variables, including ancestry, literacy, and income are given. "In a few cases, the census data were augmented with information from the U.S. Department of Agriculture and the National Council of Churches of Christ." This site is very useful for students doing reports on economic growth. For example, students living in a city that has lost population over the years can analyze why this migration from city to suburb began.

1040.com

http://www.1040.com/site/

A non-government site designed to assist with the preparation of federal income taxes. Searches include Forms & Publications, Calculators, Tax Estimator, and Online Tax Returns. Now that IRS forms are no longer mailed to taxpayers, this site becomes more critical.

Office of the Clerk, US House of Representatives

http://clerk.house.gov/

"Along with the other House officers, the Clerk is elected every two years when the House organizes for a new Congress. The majority and minority caucuses nominate candidates for the House officer positions after the election of the Speaker. The full House adopts a resolution to elect the officers, who will begin serving the Membership after they have taken the oath of office." This Web site is a complete portal for the House of Representatives. As such, it provides both current and historical information on this institution.

POW-MIA Databases

http://www.loc.gov/rr/frd/powmia-home.html

This database was established after December 1991 when the U.S. Congress enacted Public Law 102-190, the McCain Bill. "The statute requires the Secretary of Defense to make available to the public—in a 'library like setting'—all information relating to the treatment, location, and/or condition (T-L-C) of United States personnel who are unaccounted-for from the Vietnam War." This information is housed in the Library of Congress, and the Federal Research Division created the PWMIA Database, the online index to those documents. These are microfilmed documents and can be found at the Library of Congress or borrowed through local libraries. This is an official site for what is a political "hot button" issue even today.

Social Security Online

http://www.ssa.gov/

This is the official Web site of the U.S. Social Security Administration. Among other searches, you can get an estimate of your expected Social Security benefit. Individuals may also apply for Social Security and Medicare benefits through the site. Most sources suggest that you should deal with Social Security Administration through their Web site rather than face-to-face. This is particularly important for a public library.

Library of Congress Thomas Home

http://thomas.loc.gov/

On this Web site, "searching legislation, public laws or bills, and the congressional documents that pertain to the legislative process is the primary focus of Thomas. Specialized areas of the website, like the legislative process and status of appropriations, will be reviewed."

U.S. Copyright Office Search Copyright Records

http://www.copyright.gov/records/

On this Website, you can "search records of registered books, music, art, and periodicals, and other works. Includes copyright ownership documents." This site is valuable for librarians because of the material concerning digital copyright.

U.S. Patent and Trademark Office

http://www.uspto.gov/

This Web site has a number of different ways to search the database. It contains the "full text of all US patents issued since January 1, 1976, and full-page images of each page of every US patent issued since 1790." K–12 schools will not necessarily be interested in patent information but an inventor might wish to do preliminary research at the local public library.

CIA World Factbook

https://www.cia.gov/library/publications/the-world-factbook/

"The World Factbook provides information on the history, people, government, economy, geography, communications, transportation, military, and transnational issues for 267 world entities. Our Reference tab includes: maps of the major world regions, as well as Flags of the World, a Physical Map of the World, a Political Map of the World, and a Standard Time Zones of the World Map." While users may just have to set aside whatever negative thoughts they may have about the CIA, this is a great site with comprehensive information about countries of the world.

U.S. Government Printing Office

http://www.gpo.gov/fdsys/

"The core mission of Keeping America Informed, dated to 1813 when Congress determined to make information regarding the work of the three branches of Government available to all Americans. The U.S Government Printing Office (GPO) provides publishing & dissemination services for the official & authentic government publications to Congress, Federal agencies, Federal depository libraries, & the American public." The site provides digitized full-text of many GPO documents. Most librarians have had access to GPO documents through Federal Depository Libraries. The full-text feature eliminates the need to obtain documents from these depository libraries.

Country Indicators for Foreign Policy

http://www.carleton.ca/cifp/

A Canadian site, "the CIFP, a joint academic-government project, tells us we should be looking out for factors including a history of conflict, environmental stresses, ethnic divisions, and militarization, among others. A well-done interface spits out the base statistics, and irregular risk reports provide country risk ratings as well as dry, detailed country risk assessments. Reports on hot topics such as corporate social responsibility also appear on the site."

History and Politics Out Loud (HPOL)

http://www.hpol.org/

This searchable multimedia database documents and delivers authoritative audio relevant to U.S. history and politics. This project, supported by a major grant from the National Endowment for the Humanities Teaching with Technology Program, in collaboration with Michigan State University and the National Gallery of the Spoken Word, has additional Web site support from Northwestern University Library, School of Communication; Office of the Provost, Weinberg College of Arts and Sciences; and the Department of Political Science. This archive includes audio files dating back to the 1930s. Students who are preparing a U.S. history report may wish to add the actual voice(s) of persons in their reports.

International Database of the U.S. Census Bureau

http://www.census.gov/ipc/www/idb/

This database includes "global population trends, links to historical population estimates, population clocks, and estimates of population, births, and deaths occurring each year, day, hour, or second." These are statistics that library users—school, public, and academic—often need for their research and are not readily available from other sources.

Population Reference Bureau

http://www.prb.org/

"PRB informs people from around the world and in the United States about issues related to population, health, and the environment. To do this, we transform technical data and research into accurate, easy-to-understand information." This site contains similar information to that found on the International Database of the U.S. Census Bureau. I suggest that you select and use the one that you find most productive.

Property Assessment Directory

http://www.propertyassessmentdirectory.com/

Most often, property tax on real estate is levied at the county level, but it can also be levied by local government, sometimes at the municipal level. These assessments have two components, (1) the improvement or building value and (2) the land or site value. They may be given at 100 percent of value or at a lesser percentage. This database provides links to property assessment databases from around the country and the researcher can search online, by owner name or property address to find the assessed values of properties. The database also provides a few international sites. In states that have decentralized this information (such as Pennsylvania), the information is not complete. It depends on the county where the property is located.

Consumer Resources

Consumer Reports.org

http://www.consumerreports.org/cro/index.htm

The Consumers Union (CU) was founded in 1936 when advertising started to flood the mass media. At that time, consumers did not have a reliable source of information they could depend upon to help them determine hype from fact and good from bad products. This database "is an expert, independent, nonprofit organization whose mission is to work for a fair, just, and safe marketplace for all consumers and to empower consumers to protect themselves." It has a broad range of consumer information and is both independent and impartial. While Consumers Union accepts no outside advertising and no free samples, they do employ "several hundred mystery shoppers and technical experts to buy and test the products it evaluates."

Consumer Products Safety Commission (CPSC)

http://www.cpsc.gov/

The U.S. Consumer Product Safety Commission (CPSC) "is charged with protecting the public from unreasonable risks of serious injury or death from thousands of types of consumer products under the agency's jurisdiction. The CPSC is committed to protecting consumers and families from products that pose a fire, electrical, chemical, or mechanical hazard or can injure children." This agency's work in ensuring the safety of such consumer products as toys, cribs, power tools, cigarette lighters, and household chemicals has "contributed significantly to the 30 percent decline in the rate of deaths and injuries associated with consumer products over the past 30 years." Of all of the federal agencies, this information presented on this Web site seems to have little political bias.

Bankrate.com

http://www.bankrate.com/

"Bankrate, Inc. is the Web's leading aggregator of financial rate information, offering an unparalleled depth and breadth of rate data and financial content. Bankrate continually surveys approximately 4,800 financial institutions in all 50 states in order to provide clear, objective, and unbiased rates to consumers." Their website, Bankrate.com, offers free rate information to researchers on 300+ "financial products, including mortgages, credit cards, new and used automobile loans, money market accounts, certificates of deposit, checking and ATM fees, home equity loans and online banking fees."

NADA Vehicle Pricing Guides

http://www.nadaguides.com/

NADA guides were started in 2000 to offer information, products, and services to help users buy, sell, trade, or simply shop for a vehicle. Other articles and related information is available on this Web site to help vehicle owners maintain and care for the vehicles they own. For the general consumer to diehard enthusiast, "NADAguides.com is sure to have the vehicle information you're looking for. One of the most popular features of NADA guides.com is the pricing information we publish for new and used cars, trucks, vans and SUVs, as well as classic, collectible, exotic and special interest vehicles, boats, motorcycles, RVs, personal watercraft, ATVs, snowmobiles and manufactured housing." They claim to provide the most information about more types of vehicles than any other online data provider.

Kelley Blue Book

http://www.kbb.com/

"At one time, new car buyers used just MSRP as a reference point and later, the invoice price. But studies showed that there was a desire to know actual transaction prices for new cars. Kelley Blue Book went to work gathering and analyzing transactions from thousands of dealers across the United States, and in 2002, introduced kbb.com visitors to the Fair Purchase Price for new cars—what smart buyers are really paying for them." Teachers will find this Web site and that of the NADA Vehicle Pricing Guides valuable for class projects dealing with individual budgets.

Edmunds.com

http://www.edmunds.com/

"Edmunds Inc. publishes four Web sites that empower, engage and educate automotive consumers, enthusiasts and insiders. Our Web sites consist of Edmunds.com (launched in 1995 as the first automotive information Web site), *Inside Line* (launched in 2005 and the most-read automotive enthusiast Web site) and AutoObserver.com (launched in 2007 to provide insightful automotive industry commentary and analysis)." This site can be used in conjunction with the Kelly Blue Book to show students how much that car really costs and what it is worth.

NAT Tools for Good Health

http://nat.illinois.edu/

NAT, a public service of the Food Science and Human Nutrition Department at the University of Illinois, is "intended to empower individuals to select a nutrient dense diet. It is not intended to replace the advice of a physician or health professional. . . . The database used by NAT is composed of the USDA Handbook #8 and information from food companies. The data should not be taken as an exact representation of the nutrient content of your diet. The numbers used for analysis are averages and there is great variance in nutrient content for each food item in the database. The nutrient information is also not complete for every food listed in NAT as there are still gaps in our knowledge of food composition."

10

Medicine

This chapter is rather limited in resources because any examination of medical Web sites shows much material that is either dated or is something less than authoritative. Of all of the chapters in this book, this is the one that comes with a warning: Use judiciously! Many people access the Web in order to try and self-medicate and to diagnose their medical problems. In no way should the sites shown here be considered the final word on any medical issues; that is the domain of medical doctors. As with all resource chapters in the book, the description of the Web site uses the site's own words wherever possible.

PubMed Central

http://www.ncbi.nlm.nih.gov/pmc/

"PubMed Central is a free digital archive of biomedical and life sciences journal literature at the U.S. National Institutes of Health (NIH), developed and managed by NIH's National Center for Biotechnology Information (NCBI) in the National Library of Medicine (NLM). With PubMed Central, NLM has taken the lead in preserving and maintaining access to the electronic literature, just as it has done for decades with the printed biomedical literature. PubMed Central aims to fill the role of a world class library in the digital age. It is not a journal publisher. NLM believes that giving all users free access to the material in PubMed Central is the best way to ensure the durability and utility of the archive as technology changes over time." This is a very specialized archive that will probably be of much more value to academic librarians than for school and public librarians.

PubMed Home

http://www.ncbi.nlm.nih.gov/PubMed

"PubMed comprises more than 20 million citations for biomedical literature from MEDLINE, life science journals, and online books. Citations may include links to full-text content from PubMed Central and publisher web sites." Medline is a very sophisticated database, geared more for research use than for the casual home user.

CDC Wonder

http://wonder.cdc.gov/

"With CDC WONDER you can search for and read published documents on public health concerns, including reports, recommendations and guidelines, articles and statistical research data published by CDC, as well as reference materials and bibliographies on health-related topics; query numeric data sets on CDC's mainframe and other computers, via 'fill-in-the blank' web pages." This database, among many other topics available, includes public-use data sets about mortality (deaths), cancer incidence, HIV and AIDS, TB, natality (births), and census data. The requested data are readily summarized and analyzed.

"The data is ready for use in desktop applications such as word processors, spreadsheet programs, or statistical and geographic analysis packages. File formats available include web pages (HTML), chart and map images (bitmaps) and spreadsheet files (ASCII with Tab Separated Values). All of these facilities are menu-driven, and require no special computer expertise." This Web site should be particularly useful in high schools where students study health issues as well as the public library where people would like additional information about a medical diagnosis.

CHSI: Community Health Status Indicators

http://communityhealth.hhs.gov/homepage.aspx?j=1

"The goal of Community Health Status Indicators (CHSI) is to provide an overview of key health indicators for local communities and to encourage dialogue about actions that can be taken to improve a community's health. The CHSI report was designed not only for public health professionals but also for members of the community who are interested in the health of their community. The CHSI report contains over 200 measures for each of the 3,141 United States counties. Although CHSI presents indicators like deaths due to heart disease and cancer, it is imperative to understand that behavioral factors such as tobacco use, diet, physical activity, alcohol and drug use, sexual behavior and others substantially contribute to these deaths." The statistical information presented here is another example of data available on the Invisible Web that is nearly impossible to access through standard Web browsers.

Combined Health Information Database

http://pathmicro.med.sc.edu/chidmic.htm

"CHID is a database produced by health-related agencies of the Federal Government. This database provides titles, abstracts, and availability information for health information and health education resources. The value of this database is that it lists a wealth of health promotion and education materials and program descriptions that are not indexed elsewhere." New records are added to this database on a quarterly basis, and current listings are checked regularly to make sure that all entries are up-to-date and are still available from their original sources. A few older records are retained for archival purposes. Again, the information here is not indexed in many other places on the Web.

Alcohol and Alcohol Problems Science Database

http://etoh.niaaa.nih.gov/

"The National Institute on Alcohol Abuse and Alcoholism (NIAAA) has created this portal to support researchers and practitioners searching for information related to alcohol research. This page includes links to a number of databases, journals, and Web sites focused on alcohol research and related topics." This database also includes a link to the archived ETOH database which is the "premier" Alcohol and Alcohol Problems Science Database. It was produced by NIAAA from 1972 through December 2003. Although it is a fairly academic site, there are parts of it that can be of value to high school teachers and students as they discuss and research the topics of alcohol abuse and alcoholism in their classes.

FamilyDoctor.org: Health Information for the Whole Family

http://familydoctor.org/online/famdocen/home.html

"This Web site is operated by the American Academy of Family Physicians (AAFP), a national medical organization representing more than 93,700 family physicians, family practice residents and medical students." The information on this site was written and has been reviewed by physicians and patient education professionals at the AAFP. Visiting the AAFP Web site will allow your users to learn more about this organization. Links on the left of the home page provide additional information about this Web site. The AAFP also welcomes feedback if you or your teachers wish to click on the "Contact Us" link for both the e-mail and the mailing address. This is a more accessible medical database for the average user. However, the caveat mentioned in the introduction to this chapter about self-diagnosis comes into play here.

Mayo Clinic

http://www.mayoclinic.com/

"Mayo Clinic is the first and largest integrated, not-for-profit group practice in the world. Doctors from every medical specialty work together to care for patients, joined by common systems and a philosophy of 'the needs of the patient come first.'" This database would be very helpful for users who are looking for different places they might choose to go to solve a personal or family health issue.

11

Reference

The electronic references in this chapter are examples of which I can truly say are "good Web sites," especially for school libraries. The recent evolution of the reference function and school libraries has been monumental. Of all of the resources that school libraries need to provide the best sources to their students, reference materials stand as the most expensive, and the most necessary. In the earlier days of print encyclopedias, it was incumbent on the school librarian to replace one encyclopedia every year in order to have up-to-date resources. This has changed with the advent of the Internet. The electronic references mentioned in this chapter are the best I could locate and, used in conjunction with Chapter 8, Gateways, will provide thorough reference materials for school librarians and their patrons. As with all resource chapters in the book, the description of the Web site uses the site's own words wherever possible.

College Sports: Statistics and Records

http://www.ncaa.org/wps/wcm/connect/public/NCAA/Resources/Stats/index.html

"Founded more than one hundred years ago as a way to protect student-athletes, the NCAA continues to implement that principle with increased emphasis on both athletics and academic excellence." Students love this Web site because so many of them participate in athletics, and they also learn about the history of sports. Some adult users in the public library may also be interested in some of these statistics each year as "March Madness" begins.

Abbreviations and Acronym Dictionary

http://www.acronymfinder.com/

"With more than 900,000 human-edited definitions, Acronym Finder is the world's largest and most comprehensive dictionary of acronyms, abbreviations, and initialisms. Combined with the Acronym Attic, Acronym Finder contains more than 4 million acronyms and abbreviations. New! You can also search for more than 850,000 US and Canadian postal codes." The print equivalents of this information are hard to keep updated, but the electronic version does that seamlessly here.

Database of Award-Winning Children's Literature (DAWCL)

http://www.dawcl.com/

"The purpose of this database is to create a tailored reading list of quality children's literature or to find out if a book has won one of the indexed awards. I expect the user to be a librarian or a teacher intervening for a child-reader, however anyone may make use of it to find the best in children's literature including parents, book store personnel, and children and young adults themselves." This database includes 8,400 records from 96 awards presented in six English-speaking countries (United States, Canada, Australia, New Zealand, England, and Ireland). When you click the link "Explanation of Awards," you find a list of awards, their countries, and a brief explanation. Books are indexed so researchers can find them using either the form search or the keyword search. Because most awards are given every year, DAWCL remains a work in progress with addition of any new awards and new award-winners. I cannot think of an Invisible Web site that is of more value to school and public librarians for collection building and instruction.

databaseSports.com

http://www.databasesports.com/

"Our goal is to be the most comprehensive source for sports statistics and data on the internet while also providing the user with an enjoyable experience. Our focus will be on the statistics side of things but we'll also provide historical and other data for all players, leagues and teams." The database providers of this Web site plan to add new sports to this site so that it will attract an even wider audience. The sports information is very comprehensive, but there is perhaps too much emphasis on statistics than the average educator will find really useful.

Britannica Online Encyclopedia

http://www.britannica.com/

"Encyclopædia Britannica, Inc., headquartered in Chicago, Illinois, is a leading provider of learning and knowledge products. We're proud to be one of the world's most trusted sources of information on every topic imaginable—from the origins of the universe to current events and everything in between." General purpose encyclopedias have gone from fee-based to free and now back, generally speaking to fee-based. At one time this content was free to the user, but it is no longer free.

Online Encyclopedias

http://www.surfnetkids.com/encyclopedia.htm

"Although the Internet could be viewed as one giant encyclopedia, there is one very important difference: the bulk of the Internet is written by sources with dubious credentials. When you need background information for a school paper or a research project, you not only need it quickly, you need to trust your sources." This database is advertised as a trustworthy (and free) online encyclopedia. This site is strictly for K–12 (and their teachers) so do not expect in-depth coverage of any topic.

Cambridge Dictionaries Online

http://dictionary.cambridge.org/

"Cambridge University Press has been publishing dictionaries for learners of English since 1995. Cambridge Dictionaries Online has been offering these dictionaries completely free of charge since 1999.

The dictionaries that appear on Cambridge Dictionaries Online include:

• Cambridge Advanced Learner's Dictionary
• Cambridge Learner's Dictionary
• Cambridge Dictionary of American English
• Cambridge Idiom Dictionary
• Cambridge Phrasal Verb Dictionary."

Martindale's Reference Desk

http://www.martindalecenter.com/

Although based in Australia, this reference tool provides gateways to much information not accessible through regular search engines. There is so much information, but the search feature is not there at the top level.

RhymeZone

http://www.rhymezone.com/

This online tool is one of the quickest ways for a writer to choose a word if you are writing poetry, song lyrics, greeting cards, term papers, etc. It is useful to learn the relationships between words or the correct spelling of a word. "You can use it as a springboard for finding pictures, documents, and other multimedia items related to a particular concept that you're writing about. Finally, you can use it to see how your word is used in the context of famous quotes, poems, and plays." My students thought this was a great site because it provided a quick source of rhyming words, an essential thing for aspiring poets. It will appeal to the budding poet or song writer.

Pulitzer Prizes

http://www.pulitzer.org/

"The Pulitzer Prizes site contains the complete list of Pulitzer Prize winners from 1917 (the first year the Prizes were awarded) to the present. The site also lists Nominated Finalists from 1980 (the first year finalists were announced) through the present." Furthermore, this site offers the full text of Journalism winner categories after 1995 as well as selected material from winners in the Letters, Drama and Music, and Special Awards and Citations categories. From this data, you can also find biographies of winners and information on Board members and Nominating Jurors. If your students aspire to be a Pulitzer winner, they can find entry forms for the upcoming prizes, photos, press releases, and contact information for the Pulitzer Prizes office. Another use of this Web site might be the crossword puzzle fanatic who needs an answer to a clue. Please note that the site is best viewed using Internet Explorer 6.0 or later, Firefox 2.0 or later, Opera 8 or later, and Safari 3.

Universal Currency Converter

http://www.xe.com/ucc/

"XE is the world's favorite provider of Internet foreign exchange tools and services." If your school's choir is planning a spring break concert in Italy, they can determine the amount of currency they will need to translate into euros. If they pull up a menu from a restaurant in Rome, they can determine how much their meal will cost in U.S. dollars. This converter can be used with value by math and social studies teachers alike.

Biography.com

http://www.biography.com/

This is an online database with mostly brief biographies about people in all fields of endeavor. However, it would also be a good starting online point for students who have no clue as to the names they have been asked to identify.

Academy of Motion Picture Arts and Sciences

http://www.oscars.org/

"The Academy of Motion Picture Arts and Sciences is the world's preeminent movie-related organization, with a membership of more than 6,000 of the most accomplished men and women working in cinema. Although best known for its annual Oscar telecast, the Academy is involved in a wide array of education, outreach, preservation and research activities." This Web site will be very popular in February when the Oscars are presented. Students and librarians with an interest in the cinema will find this a valuable and interesting Web site.

Cyndi's List of Genealogy Sites on the Internet

http://www.cyndislist.com/

- "A categorized & cross-referenced index to genealogical resources on the Internet.
- A list of links that point you to genealogical research sites online.
- A free jumping-off point for you to use in your online research.
- A "card catalog" to the genealogical collection in the immense library that is the Internet.
- Your genealogical research portal onto the Internet."

Genealogy research has become a fast growing interest to patrons in public libraries, so you can help them begin their searches with this Web site.

FamilySearch.org

http://www.familysearch.org/eng/default.asp

"FamilySearch is the largest genealogy organization in the world. Millions of people use FamilySearch records, resources, and services to learn more about their family history. For over 100 years, FamilySearch has been actively gathering, preserving, and sharing genealogical records worldwide. Patrons may freely access our resources and service online at FamilySearch.org, or through over 4,500 family history centers in 70 countries, including the renowned Family History Library in Salt Lake City, Utah." Because this Web site accesses the immense and thorough Mormon genealogy database, I find it most valuable.

Social Security Death Index

http://ssdi.rootsweb.ancestry.com/

Sometimes death dates can be hard-to-find resources. A free search on this Web site provides both name and death date, along with the name of the state where the deceased was living at the time of death.

Phone Book

http://www.thephonebook.bt.com/publisha.content/en/search/residential/search.publisha

This is a very complete residential phone book and will be much needed as printed phone books are eventually phased-out.

12

Science and Mathematics

Much of the material on the Internet and the World Wide Web is about mathematics and the sciences. This is one of the two most extensive chapters in the book (Chapter 13, Social Sciences and the Humanities being larger) dealing with the Invisible Web resources. As with all resource chapters in the book, the description of the Web site uses the site's own words wherever possible. This chapter is divided into nine sections: Mathematics, General Science, Nature, Biology, Chemistry, Computer Science, Earth Science, Space, and Weather.

MATHEMATICS

Online Encyclopedia of Integer Sequences (OEIS)

http://oeis.org/

A student at Cornell, Neal J.A. Sloan, was curious about number sequences and he became NJAS. The history of this transformation can be found on the OEIS Foundation Web site and may appeal to students interested in integer sequences. In 2009, NJAS created a non-profit foundation, The OEIS Foundation Inc., to "own, maintain and raise funds to support The On-Line Encyclopedia of Integer Sequences™ (OEIS™)." NJAS transferred the intellectual property of OEIS from NJAS to the newly created foundation on October 26, 2009 and the database moved NJAS's home page at AT&T to a commercial hosting service. At this time, two versions of the database are available: the "classic" OEIS (a continuation of the version that was on NJAS's home page) and a moderated Wiki. As with most of the entries in this chapter, this site is for math teachers rather than for students.

The Math Forum: Ask Dr. Math

http://mathforum.org/dr/math/

Ask Dr. Math, a question-and-answer service for math students and their teachers, is an archive searchable by level and topic, as well as summaries of Frequently Asked Questions, or the Dr. Math FAQ. Students who wish to submit questions to Dr. Math must fill out their Web form. Answers are returned by e-mail. The best questions and answers are transferred into a searchable archive organized by grade level (elementary, middle school, high school) and topic (exponents, infinity, polynomials, etc.). You can use the Dr. Math searcher to find what you want through keywords and you can investigate the Dr. Math FAQ for topics such as prime numbers and *pi*.

SCIENCE GENERAL

Energy Files: Energy Science and Technology Virtual Library

http://pubsci.osti.gov/

"At this site you will find over 500 databases and Web sites containing information and resources pertaining to science and technology of interest to the Department of Energy, with an emphasis on the physical sciences." The Office of Scientific and Technical Information (OSTI) within the Department of Energy sponsors, develops, and maintains EnergyFiles. With its information, tools, and technologies, EnergyFiles provide access to scientific resources so that your students will be able to use these resources. This Web site has sophisticated information probably best suited for academic libraries.

E-print Network: Energy, Science, and Technology for the Research Community!

http://www.osti.gov/eprints/

"A vast, integrated network of electronic scientific and technical information created by scientists and research engineers active in their respective fields, all full-text searchable. E-print Network is intended for use by other scientists, engineers, and students at advanced levels." The database provides a gateway to over 34,000 websites and databases worldwide. With this access, your students will have access to over 5.5 million e-prints in basic and applied sciences. While the database primarily covers physics, it also has chemistry, biology and life sciences, materials science, nuclear sciences and engineering, energy research, computer and information technologies, and other disciplines of interest to the U.S. Department of Energy.

Query Nuclear Explosions Database

http://www.ga.gov.au/oracle/nuclear-explosion.jsp

"Geoscience Australia maintains a database of nuclear explosions with the location, time and size of explosions around the world since 1945. You can query this database by it brings a wide, wide range of scientific knowledge filling in the form on the homepage." There is good information on this Web site, but it requires a good amount of knowledge about nuclear weapons and nuclear testing to get useful results.

ScienceCentral.com

http://www.sciencecentral.com

This Web site includes a vast directory of science databases and sites that provides both deep and wide coverage of all aspects of science. All databases are searchable and are full text. I love this site because it brings a wide range of scientific knowledge into one place to allow for easy searching. It is equally valuable for teachers, students, and librarians.

Information Bridge

http://www.osti.gov/bridge/

"The Information Bridge: DOE Scientific and Technical Information provides free public access to over 259,000 full-text documents and bibliographic citations of Department of Energy (DOE) research report literature. Documents are primarily from 1991 forward and were produced by DOE, the DOE contractor community, and/or DOE grantees. Legacy documents are added as they become available in electronic format." This database provides a collection of documents and citations in physics, chemistry, materials, biology, environmental sciences, energy technologies, engineering, computer and information science, and renewable energy, among other disciplines.

lanl.arXiv.org.

http://xxx.lanl.gov/

This database is owned, operated, and funded by a not-for-profit educational institution, Cornell University. There is now a Facebook link for the site. "arXiv is an e-print service in the fields of physics, mathematics, non-linear science, computer science, quantitative biology, quantitative finance and statistics. Any submissions to arXiv must conform to Cornell University academic standards."

Research is an essential part of the scientific process and this database provides much useful research information.

Monthly Energy Review

http://www.eia.doe.gov/mer/

"The Monthly Energy Review (MER) is the U.S. Energy Information Administration's primary report of recent energy statistics. Included are total energy production, consumption, and trade; energy prices; overviews of petroleum, natural gas, coal, electricity, nuclear energy, renewable energy, and international petroleum; carbon dioxide emissions; and data unit conversions."

Nuclear Power Plant Databases

http://www.insc.anl.gov/

"The INSC Database provides an interactively-accessible information resource and communications medium for researchers and scientists engaged in projects sponsored by the INSC. Major portions of the INSC Database are devoted to nuclear plant-specific information, material properties for safety and risk analyses, INSC project documentation, and project-specific reactor safety bibliographies." While much of the information in this database is open to the public, information which is preliminary or proprietary is not published. Closed information can be accessed only with permission. With alternative energy sites becoming more numerous, the debate had arisen again about the safety of nuclear power. Certainly, the nuclear crisis in Japan after the earthquake and the tsunami will generate much continuing discussion about this topic, and students will be interested in getting information for science class discussions or for any research paper they might be asked to write.

Scirus for Scientific Information

http://www.scirus.com/

"Scirus is the most comprehensive scientific research tool on the web. With over 410 million scientific items indexed at last count, it allows researchers to search for not only journal content but also scientists' homepages, courseware, pre-print server material, patents and institutional repository and website information." This database offers sophisticated information aimed at academics.

Sun or Moon Rise/Set Table for One Year: U.S. Cities and Towns

http://www.usno.navy.mil/USNO/astronomical-applications/data-services/rs-one-year-us

This database has a form that helps the user find a table of the times of sunrise/sunset, moonrise/moonset, or the beginning and end of twilight, for one year. It covers U.S. cities and towns only. For any other locations in the United States or worldwide, the user must add the latitude and longitude. Instructions are as shown below.

- "Enter the year for which the table is desired.
- Select the table type (sunrise/sunset, moonrise/moonset, etc.) from the pop-up list.
- Specify the location of interest.
- Click the 'Compute Table' button at the end of the form to compute the table. The table will provide the data requested in local standard time on a 24-hour clock; for example, 1836 means 6:36 p.m., local standard time."

Galileo Project

http://galileo.rice.edu/science.html

"Here you can find records of the other scientists and scientific institutions of Galileo's time, as well as information about Galileo's astronomical observations and instruments. Additionally, you can access a document from the University of Bologna's Astronomical Museum about 17th century astronomical instruments." This is a really neat site that appeals to students because of the site's role playing and animation features. Not an avatar, but a lot of role playing is possible here.

Scientific World Journal

http://www.thescientificworld.com/TSW/main/home.asp?ocr=1&jid=141

"TheScientificWorld was founded to grow and develop the suite of innovative publications of TheScientificWorld. Through its range of e-journal and e-book publications, TSW offers high quality peer-reviewed original research and review articles to researchers and librarians in academia, government and the corporate world." The information is free but the site requires registration.

UFO Seek: The UFO Paranormal Search Engine, News, Forums

http://www.ufoseek.com/

"UFOseek.com was founded in 1998 as a human-edited 'UFO phenomenon' search engine and directory dedicated to UFO, Paranormal, Religious, Spiritual and unexplainable subjects. Over the years Ufoseek became very large and popular UFO paranormal directory on the web. You can submit your UFO or paranormal site to Ufoseek for free. However, we only index quality sites with related UFO, paranormal content." UFOseek will appeal to your students who want to study UFOs and it is tremendous tool for those doing research. Users can post UFO images, video, their UFO sightings, or their paranormal experiences.

Another part of this service is UFOseek News, a source of the latest news on UFO Conspiracies, UFO Photographs, UFO Sightings, UFO Theories, Alien Abductions, Paranormal, Area 51, Space Science, NASA, Astronomy, among other topics. Whether you believe in UFOs or not, your students will find this site to make for engrossing reading.

NATURE

African Elephant Database

http://www.african-elephant.org/aed/index.html

"The AESR 2007 presents the latest information on elephant population estimates and range at the site, national, regional and continental levels.... New tables assist in interpreting the possible reasons why estimates have changed since the previous edition; comparisons are made for methodologically comparable estimates at the regional level; and a system for prioritizing has been developed to guide governments and funding agencies in planning future surveys." While students in the United States might have a great deal of difficulty imaging herds of elephants, the process of this type of survey could be transferred to surveys of buffalo or polar bears on their own continent.

Biological Inventories of the World's Protected Areas

http://www.ice.ucdavis.edu/bioinventory/bioinventory.html

This database was developed by The Information Center for the Environment (ICE), a part of the Department of Environmental Science & Policy at the University of California, Davis. Numerous collaborators helped in developing databases "containing documented, taxonomically harmonized species inventories of plants and animals reported from the world's protected areas." This allows students and teachers access to information "that is otherwise largely unavailable via the internet and provide a mechanism for protected areas and protected area systems to publish their species inventories when they would otherwise be unable to do so." With the focus of many groups on saving endangered plants and animals, this site would help them choose a species to "protect."

ENature.com Field Guides

http://www.enature.com/fieldguides/

"eNature.com is the web's premier destination for information about the wild animals and plants of the United States. Over past years, eNature has consistently been one of the Internet's most-visited sites for nature and wildlife information and has won numerous awards and accolades." The core content of wildlife information on this database has almost 6,000 individual species, the same data set was used to create the printed *Audubon Field Guides*. Leading biologists, zoologists, and other natural history specialists carefully reviewed all the data. This database is owned and operated by the Shearwater Marketing Group, a privately-held company "that provides marketing services to both non-profit and private sector clients, focusing primarily on wildlife and nature." While this has great content for science teachers and students, the site is somewhat commercial because of this connection.

FishBase

http://www.fishbase.org/search.php

"The FishBase and SeaLifeBase teams are proud to offer as public goods a wide variety of interfaces to the underlying databases. We regularly add new tools, lists and queries that we deem useful or those that have been requested by our users, and design on request simple queries to create original datasets for research purposes."

NatureServe: Explorer: An Online Encyclopedia of Life

http://www.natureserve.org/explorer/

"NatureServe Explorer provides conservation status, taxonomy, distribution, and life history information for more than 70,000 plants, animals, and ecological communities and systems in the United States and Canada....The data available through NatureServe Explorer represent a 'snapshot' of the U.S. and Canadian data managed in the NatureServe Central Databases." Hundreds of natural heritage program scientists and other collaborators offer input to these databases. The database is "periodically updated from these central databases to reflect information from new field surveys, the latest taxonomic treatments and other scientific publications, and new conservation status assessments." In my view, these updates are somewhat too infrequent. In order to have more value, the updates should be done more frequently. However, this is a comment that reflects what I would want, not the reality of updating a complex Web site.

The IUCN Red List of Threatened Species

http://www.iucnredlist.org/

"The IUCN Red List of Threatened Species™ is widely recognized as the most comprehensive, objective global approach for evaluating the conservation status of plant and animal species. From its small beginning, the IUCN Red List has grown in size and complexity and now plays an increasingly prominent role in guiding conservation activities of governments, NGOs and scientific institutions." In 1994, a scientifically rigorous approach was introduced to determine risks of extinction that is applicable to all species, and this has become a world standard. This database is produced by individuals working with the IUCN Survival Commission (SSC) and with members of IUCN who draw on and mobilize a network of scientists and partner organizations from almost every country in the world. This is considered one of the most complete scientific knowledge bases on the biology and conservation status of species.

BIOLOGY

Gene Cards Version 3

http://www.genecards.org/

"GeneCards is a searchable, integrated, database of human genes that provides concise genomic related information on all known and predicted human genes....The GeneCards human gene database extracts and integrates a carefully selected subset of gene related transcriptomic, genetic, proteomic, functional and disease information, from dozens of relevant sources." The database allows user-friendly access to up-to-date knowledge using "standard nomenclature and approved gene symbols." A complete summary is given for each gene and students can gain "a deep understanding of biology and medicine."

Integrated Taxonomic Information System (IT IS) Biological Informatics Program

http://biology.usgs.gov/bio/itis.html

"The goal for ITIS is to create an easily accessible database with reliable information on species names and their hierarchical classification. The database is reviewed periodically to ensure high quality with valid classifications, revisions, and additions of newly described species. ITIS includes documented taxonomic information of flora and fauna from both aquatic and terrestrial habitats." While the primary focus of this database has been on native North American species, it also includes thousands of non-native species from other continents. ITIS anticipates that geographic coverage will eventually be worldwide through their relationships with several national and international biodiversity programs.

In teaching the use of this database, students will be able to find the authority (author and date), taxonomic rank, associated synonyms and vernacular names where available, a unique taxonomic serial number, data source information (publications, experts, etc.) for each species. The database also offers data quality indicators, expert reviews, and changes to taxonomic information in the database. Based on the AP Biology curriculum for high schools, this site will be of particular value to students enrolled in this class.

PLANTS Database

http://plants.usda.gov/java/

"The PLANTS Database provides standardized information about the vascular plants, mosses, liverworts, hornworts, and lichens of the U.S. and its territories. It includes names, plant symbols, checklists, distributional data, species abstracts, characteristics, images, crop information, automated tools, onward Web links, and references." While this information was designed to promote land conservation in the United States and its territories, it will also be useful for academic, educational, and general use. The designers believe that this database, by minimizing duplication and making information exchange possible, reduces government spending.

Chemistry

ChemBioFinder.com

http://www.chemfinder.com/chembiofinder/Forms/Home/ContentArea/Home.aspx

ChemBioFinder.com, an online chemistry and biology reference database, indexes and links more than 500,000 compounds to other Web sites providing a wealth of chemical information for professional chemists and students. This database is the gateway to all databases available from CambridgeSoft. "A subscriber can search for compounds by name, CAS Registry Number, molecular formula or weight, or by structure (exact and substructure). Successful searches return a basic profile of molecules indexed by this site. The profile contains the name, molecular formula and weight, CAS Registry Number, SMILES and InChI strings." The databases are listed which contain entries for the located compound(s). While free trials are available to any of these databases, an annual subscription is needed for continuous use of the contents.

NIST Chemistry Web Book

http://webbook.nist.gov/chemistry/

This Web site was created by the National Institute of Standards and Technology (NIST). It provides thermochemical, thermophysical, and ion energetics data compiled under the Standard Reference Data Program. NIST "uses its best efforts to deliver a high quality copy of the Database and to verify that the data contained therein have been selected on the basis of sound scientific judgment. However, NIST makes no warranties to that effect, and NIST shall not be liable for any damage that may result from errors or omissions in the Database." This site would be primarily for teachers and academic libraries because of the complexity of the material.

ChemWeb

http://www.chemweb.com/

"Journal Abstracts from chemistry publishers such as Bentham, Elsevier, Springer and others covering over 500 journals can be searched and accessed for free. Search by title and issue or use Journal Search for full-text search of abstracts across all journals." Membership to register for ChemWeb.com is free and the database provides access to chemical information needed to enhance research, develop products, self-development, and education in Chemistry and related disciplines. Easy access is provided to abstracts, papers, books, conferences, news, forums and the Alchemt newsletter. Members also "have exclusive content access and can participate in the many ChemWeb community features."

COMPUTER SCIENCE

ACM Digital Library

http://portal.acm.org/dl.cfm

This science Web site contains the "full text of every article ever published by ACM and bibliographic citations from major publishers in computing." Membership in ACM is required, but at the university level, many university professors may already be members.

Bitpipe.com

http://www.bitpipe.com/

"Bitpipe.com is the enterprise IT professional's guide to information technology resources. Browse this free online library for the latest technical white papers, webcasts and product information to help you make intelligent IT product purchasing decisions."

Microsoft Support

http://support.microsoft.com/

"Find Solutions to your technical problems in our Support Solution Center. To get started, click the Solutions Center button." If you love or hate Microsoft, there is much good, free information on this Web site, such as tutorials for different pieces of Microsoft software.

NetLingo

http://www.netlingo.com/

"With more than 82 million people texting regularly, it's no wonder you've seen this cryptic looking code! Commonly used wherever people get online—

including IMing, SMSing, cell phones, Blackberries, PDAs, Web sites, games, newsgroup postings, in chat rooms, on blogs—these abbreviations are used by people to communicate with each other. The actual definition of an acronym and text shorthand is here."

EARTH SCIENCES

Antarctic Research Atlas

http://lima.usgs.gov/antarctic_research_atlas/

This Web site has been "developed by the USGS Information Access and Data Delivery project at the USGS EROS Data Center." This is a quite specialized Web site, generally not of value for students. It would be most utile to faculty and researchers.

National Institute for Environmental Studies Database

http://www.nies.go.jp/db/index-e.html

Many research reports are found on this Web site with some available for downloading in PDF file format. "In addition, all research reports can be viewed in the Institute's library (duplication service is not provided). Regarding printed reports, we distribute copies if they are in stock. Please contact the Environmental Information Center (facsimile 81-298-50-2566). The cost of mailing the reports will be charged."

Earthquake Search

http://earthquake.usgs.gov/earthquakes/eqarchives/epic/

Provided by the U.S. Geological Survey's (USGS) Earthquake Hazards Program, this database is part of USGS' effort to reduce earthquake hazard in the United States. Is is part of the USGS Geologic Discipline and is the USGS's component of the congressionally established, multi-agency National Earthquake Hazards Reduction Program (NEHRP). "The USGS participates in the NEHRP with the Federal Emergency Management Agency (FEMA), the National Institute of Standards and Technology (NIST), and the National Science Foundation (NSF)." When NEHRP by was reauthorized by Congress, NIST was given the lead role in planning and coordinating "this national effort to mitigate earthquake losses by developing and applying earth science data and assessments essential for land-use planning, engineering design, and emergency preparedness decisions." Again, the earthquake/tsunami disaster in Japan in 2011 will make the information in this database valuable to science teachers and students.

EE-Link Is Environmental Education on the Internet

http://eelink.net/pages/EE-Link+Introduction

"EE-Link is 5800 links organized in 300 categories, 11,000+ visitors per day. Browse or Search for resources for professional development, climate change, global warming, lesson plans, endangered species, national and international events, jobs, activities for the classroom, and more." This is an excellent site for science teachers. The information found here can be invaluable. Environmental education is rapidly becoming a prominent part in K–12 curricula and this database is a valuable supplement to other class materials.

Home Envirofacts

http://www.epa.gov/envirofw/

This Envirofacts Multisystem Search Web site brings together information from a variety of databases and includes latitude and longitude information. Each of these databases contains "information about facilities that are required to report activity to a state or federal system." Students can retrieve information about hazardous waste (including the Biennial Report), toxic and air releases. This Web site also contains lists of "Superfund sites, and water discharge permits. Facility information and a map of its location is provided."

Incident News

http://www.incidentnews.gov/

"The Incident News website provides publicly available information related to oil and hazardous material spills, both current and historical. It is developed and maintained by NOAA's Emergency Response Division (ERD), which is part of NOAA's Office of Response and Restoration (OR&R). ERD was formerly known as the Hazardous Materials Response Division, or HAZMAT." The information provided on this site is scary! Many more incidents occur than we are aware of until a huge oil spill such as the unfortunate BP disaster in the Gulf of Mexico comes to the attention of the media.

Abandoned Mine Land Inventory System (AMLIS)

http://www.osmre.gov/aml/amlis/amlis.shtm

"The Abandoned Mine Land Inventory System is a computer system used to store, manage, and report on the Office of Surface Mining's Inventory of Abandoned Mine Land Problems. This includes both problems in need of reclamation and those that have been reclaimed."

Right-to-Know Network (RTK NET)

http://www.rtknet.org/

The Right-to-Know Network offers free access to numerous databases and resources on the environment. With the information available here, students and faculty can "identify specific factories and their environmental effects; find permits issued under environmental statutes; and identify civil cases filed." This database is free and it was established "in order to empower citizen involvement in community and government decision-making."

Mineral Resources On-Line Spatial Data

http://mrdata.usgs.gov/

This Web site provides "interactive maps and downloadable data for regional and global Geology, Geochemistry, Geophysics, and Mineral Resources."

Volcano Data at NGDC

http://www.ngdc.noaa.gov/hazard/volcano.shtml

"NGDC acquires and disseminates volcano data and images of volcanoes in eruption." The images could be useful to elementary teachers who cover volcanoes in their science lessons.

World Lake Database

http://wldb.ilec.or.jp/

"We currently have data for more than 500 lakes from 73 countries in World Lake Database. These data mainly consists of result of a data collection project entitled "Survey of the State of World Lakes" in cooperation with the United Nations Environment Programme (UNEP). Geography is an overlooked part of many school curricula and this site provides a good supplement to those curricula.

SPACE

Earth from Space

http://earth.jsc.nasa.gov/sseop/efs/

Selected photos and related captions are uploaded to the Internet in order to allow users a glimpse of this national treasure. This database was compiled to illustrate interesting Earth features and processes and includes images of cities as seen by astronauts from space. You have several choices to search for selected images. "Each image is available in three resolutions and includes cataloging data and a caption. However, this site contains only a small selection of the best of our Earth photography. The complete database of NASA's Earth imagery is available at the Gateway to Astronaut Photography of Earth, which contains 1,048,018 images (count updated 1/1/2011)." The images are breathtaking for all searchers.

Solar System Simulator

http://space.jpl.nasa.gov/

"The Solar System Simulator originated as JPL's SPACE software package, which consisted of a set of computer graphics programs designed to simulate spacecraft trajectories and produce various photographic and video products. The SPACE package was specifically designed for animating space missions and was uniquely suited to JPL mission design."

WEATHER

National Climatic Data Center

http://www.ncdc.noaa.gov/oa/ncdc.html

"The basic tenet of physical climate data management at NOAA is full and open data access. All raw physical climate data available from NOAA's various climate observing systems as well as the output data from state-of-the-science climate models are openly available in as timely a manner as possible." Just how timely the data is depends upon when it is received and the quality control procedures needed to confirm that the data are valid. The latest versions of derived data sets are also made available to the public as well as access to all of its major climate-related model simulations.

Weatherbase

http://www.weatherbase.com/

"WeatherbaseSM is your one authoritative source for finding monthly weather records and averages for more than 16,439 cities worldwide. Climatological information is one of the most sought-after areas of weather information by Internet users." Students and faculty can use it for personal advance event planning, finding vacation spots, and simply to satisfy curiosity. This database provides a comprehensive weather resource center, a weather glossary, and Vacation Finder. It is a unique planning technology locating places to visit based on the average weather in cities worldwide.

13

Social Science and Humanities

This chapter about the social sciences and the humanities turned out to be the most extensive in the book and literally goes from a to z. Some of the material is government-based, but it still falls within this chapter. The extensive databases in the Web sites presented here should assist librarians, teachers, students, and the researcher alike. As with all resource chapters in the book, the description of the Web site uses the site's own words wherever possible. This chapter is divided into nine sections: General Social Sciences, Diversity, History, Music, News, Religion, Transportation and Travel, Geography and Maps, and Law.

GENERAL SOCIAL SCIENCES

Anthropology Review Database (ARD)

http://wings.buffalo.edu/ARD/cgi/modbio.cgi?submit=See+The+Bios

"The Anthropology Review Database is intended to improve the level of access of anthropologists to anthropological literature by making them more aware of what is being published and helping them to evaluate its relevance to their own interests. Unlike the more traditional print journals, ARD is not constrained by production deadlines and has few running costs." The Web site creators feel they can keep abreast of the production of new materials in a more timely fashion than traditional media. This is one of those Web sites geared towards professionals rather than students.

Central Intelligence Agency Freedom of Information Act (FOIA) Electronic Reading Room

http://www.foia.cia.gov/

"The FOIA Electronic Reading Room is provided as a public service by the CIA and its Office of Information Management. Here you can view previously released documents, released through the FOIA and other disclosure statutes." To view previously released documents and collections, students and teachers can visit three locations, the Frequently Requested Records, Special Collections, and the 25 Year Program Archive. To search documents, users will find the search bar at the top of the page or they can browse collections of documents on historically significant topics. Furthermore, the CIA must comply with U.S. national security laws, and some documents or parts of documents are not released to the public. This means that you will get some documents that have been extensively blacked out.

Military Images

http://www.military.com/Resources/ResourceSubmittedFileView?file=multimedia_images.htm

"Military.com provides headline news and technology updates since our community answers the call and makes news. We also cover the rest of the military experience—from great content like our user-generated videos in our popular "Shock and Awe" feature to our military equipment guide we present what makes the military unique (and fun)." Students really like the images that are presented here, and they will also like to include them in their reports about military topics. The military is a popular topic among many students and this site provides the images they will want to use.

U.S. Copyright Office

http://www.copyright.gov/

This Web site was created for the copyright community of creators and users, as well as for the general public. While information is shared about the online registration option and other news about reengineering, all the key publications including "informational circulars; application forms for copyright registration; links to the copyright law and to the homepages of other copyright-related organizations; a link to our online copyright records cataloged since 1978; news of what the Office is doing, including business process reengineering plans, Congressional testimony, and press releases; our latest regulations; and much more" are here.

Gender Statistics Web Site

http://www.unece.org/stats/gender/

This interesting site includes data from the United Nations and shows the wide range of gender information from around the world. It links gender issues to statistical indicators created by the UNECE/UNDP gender statistics task force. This UNECE Gender Statistics Database helps to monitor the situation of women and men in all UNECE member countries, and provide evidence to evaluate the effectiveness of policies. This Web site is aimed more at professionals using academic or public libraries.

Humanities Resources on the Invisible Web

http://websearch.about.com/od/invisibleweb/a/invisiblewebart.htm

About.com offers nearly 800 guides to help users find solutions to a wide range of daily needs. Some examples of informational resources are parenting, health care, technology, cooking, travel, and many others. This database has about 40 million (average) unique visitors in the United States and another 75 million visitors worldwide. Statistics show that 80 percent of users come to the database from search engines, seeking solutions in response to moments of need. The database is continually updated and covers more than 70,000 sources with 6,000 pieces of new content added each week.

DIVERSITY

CLAS: Culturally & Linguistically Appropriate Services

http://clas.uiuc.edu/

The CLAS Early Childhood Research Institute, in collaboration with colleagues with diverse cultural and linguistic roots, collects and describes "early childhood/early intervention resources that have been developed across the U.S. for children with disabilities and their families and the service providers who work with them." Materials and resources found here reflect the intersection of culture and language, disabilities and child development. "Through this site we intend to inform consumers (e.g., practitioners, families, and researchers) about materials and practices that are available and the contexts in which they might select a given material or practice." Some of the site can be read in Spanish.

HISTORY

American Memory from the Library of Congress

http://memory.loc.gov/ammem/index.html

The American Memory project from the Library of Congress offers free and open access through the Internet to written and spoken words, sound recordings, still and moving images, prints, maps, and sheet music documenting the U.S. experience, a digital record of U.S. history and creativity. Uploaded from the collections of the Library of Congress and other institutions, the content provides historical events, people, places, and ideas that continue to shape the United States. This is an excellent resource for students, teachers, and the public. The American memory site was always a favorite of AP American history teachers. This site is somewhat difficult to search, but the results are ultimately rewarding.

Avalon Project: Documents in Law, History and Diplomacy

http://avalon.law.yale.edu/default.asp

The Avalon Project is designed to provide digital documents relevant to the fields of Law, History, Economics, Politics, Diplomacy, and Government. They offer text, but also add value to this text by linking any supporting documents which are referred to in the body of the text. Users are warned that this site may offer controversial documents with the disclaimer that "Their inclusion does not indicate endorsement of their contents nor sympathy with the ideology, doctrines, or means employed by their authors. They are included for the sake of completeness and balance and because in many cases they are by our definition a supporting document." This is a "tried and true" site dealing with the law.

HarpWeek Explore History

http://www.harpweek.com/

This unusual database was created by a dozen indexers with advanced degrees. Beginning in 1995, these indexers read every word and studied every illustration and cartoon in *Harper's Weekly*. Their user-friendly indexes provide quick and concise access to the content. "The information is presented in an easy-to-navigate, alphabetical, multi-level structure familiar to scholars, reference librarians and students alike. Descriptive sub-entries will help you determine the relative value of the references by giving you specific information about an entry prior to display." This fifty-six years of the magazine's history has provided a continuous record of what happened on a weekly basis from 1857 through 1912 with eight segments. The first segment includes the Civil War Era: 1857–1865; segments two and three includes Reconstruction: 1866–1871 and 1872–1877 while the last six segments include the Gilded Age: 1878–1912.

Lincoln/Net

http://lincoln.lib.niu.edu/aboutinfo.html

The product of the American Lincoln Historical Digitization Project, Lincoln/ Net is based at Northern Illinois University; however the Lincoln Project works with a number of Illinois institutions, including the University of Chicago, the

Newberry Library, the Chicago Historical Society, Illinois State University, the Illinois State Archives, Lewis University, and Knox College. These collaborating institutions have contributed their historical materials, including books, manuscripts, images, maps and other resources, to the Lincoln Project. These may be examined in several ways. (This is a part of the project to digitize all of Lincoln's writings.) "Lincoln/Net users may search all materials in the archives using this site's search engine. Project staff have also gathered these materials together into groups containing similar materials. Site users may restrict their research to specific media types, browsing or searching through textual materials, images and maps, sound recordings, video materials, and interactive resources."

Making of America (MoA)

http://quod.lib.umich.edu/m/moagrp/

A digital library of primary sources in U.S. social history from the Antebellum Period through Reconstruction, the MoA collection is strong in the subject areas of education, psychology, American history, sociology, religion, and science and technology. "The collection currently contains approximately 10,000 books and 50,000 journal articles with 19th century imprints." This Web site is valuable for researchers wanting to deal with primary resources.

National Register of Historic Places

http://www.nps.gov/history/nr/

"The National Register of Historic Places is the official list of the Nation's historic places worthy of preservation. Authorized by the National Historic Preservation Act of 1966, the National Park Service's National Register of Historic Places is part of a national program to coordinate and support public and private efforts to identify, evaluate, and protect America's historic and archeological resources."

This next database will require someone who can read Greek if not classical Greek.

Perseus Digital Library

http://www.perseus.tufts.edu/hopper/

The Perseus Digital Library publishes TEI XML digital editions for Plutarch, Athenaeus, the Greek Anthology, Elegy and Iambus and for most of Lucian, increasing the available Plutarch from roughly 100,000 to the surviving 1,150,000 words. The Athenaeus and the Greek Anthology have been added to this database with roughly 270,000 and 160,000 words of Greek. "The 13,000 words for J.M. Edmonds Elegy and Iambus include both the surviving poetic quotations and major contexts in which these poems are quoted. The

200,000 words of Lucian represent roughly 70% of the surviving works attributed to that author. In all, this places more than 1.6 million words of Greek in circulation." The site can have value for students and teachers through college, but would be of primary benefit for classics students.

MUSIC

Music Education Search System

http://129.171.228.57/fmi/xsl/MESS/index.xsl

"The Music Education Search System was developed and is maintained by Edward P. Asmus, Ph.D. as a service to the music education community." Three databases comprise the system as detailed below, and they are most useful because of the paucity of information on the Visible Net about music education. Your music educators will be delighted to learn about this site.

1. Music Journals

At present, this database site has more than 20,000 entries.

2. Poland-Cady Abstract Collection

In the late 1960s, William Poland and Henry Cady of The Ohio State University collection gathered more than 4,500 entries. The creators used a federal grant to collect and abstract important writings in the field of music education written prior to 1965. The database contains author, title, source, and abstract information for each of the citations the authors identified.

3. Boletin De Investigacio Educativo Musical

"The Boletin is the most important music education research journal in Latin America. The database contains author, title, source, and abstract information in English. The journal contains both English and Spanish translations of the articles."

Operabase

http://www.operabase.com/

This database offers information on performances, artists, managers, and companies. For performances, searches are available for over 40,000 opera performances since August 2009. You can check the annotated list of coming highlights, or browse the listings of over 200 festivals. If you are interested in artists, you search for a specific artist and then you will find links to performance details, repertoire, biographies, and pictures. The list of artist managers has contact information and rosters while "companies" includes opera houses and festivals by name or address, or by using the mouse-sensitive maps.

Mudcat Discussion Forum

http://www.mudcat.org/

While researching a song, the researcher might find it in the Digital Tradition Folk Song Database. While a request can be posted, visitors are asked to use the search box in the upper-left corner of the first page (and most other Mudcat pages) to find the database and forum for the lyrics before you ask for help. The database contains about 9,000 folk songs. If the song the student is seeking is not in the database, their search engine will also search the forum for songs that have not been added to the database. If a folk song is missing from the database or forum, "start a new thread [click here to create a thread (topic)], and make sure the title or a phrase from the song you want is in the thread title."

Mutopia Project

http://www.mutopiaproject.org/

The Mutopia Project offers free download of sheet music editions of classical music from editions in the public domain. Included are works by well-known composers such as Bach, Beethoven, Chopin, Handel, Mozart, and many others. A team of volunteers typeset the music by computer using the LilyPond software.

NEWS

Bloomberg Business and Financial News

http://www.bloomberg.com/

"In 1981 Bloomberg started out with one core belief: that bringing transparency to capital markets through access to information could increase capital flows, produce economic growth and jobs, and significantly reduce the cost of doing business. Today, this database builds on that foundation and tries to connect decision makers in business, finance and government to a network of information, news, people and ideas that is both broad and dynamic and that enables users to make faster, more effective decisions."

CNN. com

http://www.cnn.com/

"CNN.com is among the world's leaders in online news and information delivery. Staffed 24 hours, seven days a week by a dedicated staff in CNN's world headquarters in Atlanta, Georgia, and in bureaus worldwide, CNN.com relies heavily on CNN's global team of almost 4,000 news professionals." This database features the latest multimedia technologies including live video streaming and audio packages as well as searchable archives of news features and background information. A true feature of this site is that it is updated continuously throughout the day making it a first stop for the most current news content.

Newspapersonline.com

http://www.newspapersonline.com/

This Web site allows you to locate online newspapers, local newspapers, or world news. It also has an extensive newspaper directory.

NPR: National Public Radio

http://www.npr.org/

"The mission of NPR is to work in partnership with member stations to create a more informed public—one challenged and invigorated by a deeper understanding and appreciation of events, ideas and cultures." NPR produces, acquires, and distributes programming that meets "the highest standards of public service in journalism and cultural expression." NPR also offers satellite interconnection for the entire public radio system. NPR is a popular radio network and this site supplements their programming.

Legacy.com-Obituaries

http://www.legacy.com/NS/

"Founded in 1998, Legacy.com is an innovative online media company that collaborates with more than 800 newspapers in North America, Europe and Australia to provide ways for readers to express condolences and share remembrances of loved ones." This database is visited by more than 14 million users each month. Creators have partnerships with 124 of the 150 largest newspapers in the United States. It also features obituaries and Guest Books for more than two-thirds of the people who die in the United States. This fascinating database allows the user to find out about how we memorialize the dead.

Paper of Record

http://www.paperofrecord.com/default.asp

"With 21 million images in our collection so far, PaperofRecord.com is looking to a multi-billion-newspaper page universe to create a resource that will be used by scholars, students and individuals of all walks of life, for generations to come." This is a good source that has been bedeviled by technical issues. Often the login procedure would not work and at other times material that was to be available was not.

Television News Archive

http://tvnews.vanderbilt.edu/

"The Vanderbilt Television News Archive is the world's most extensive and complete archive of television news. We have been recording, preserving and providing access to television news broadcasts of the national networks since August 5, 1968." This database spans the presidential administrations of Lyndon Johnson, Richard Nixon, Gerald Ford, Jimmy Carter, Ronald Reagan, George H.W. Bush, Bill Clinton, George W. Bush, and Barack Obama. Its core collection includes evening news broadcasts from the three major networks: ABC, CBS, and NBC (since 1968), an hour per day of CNN (since 1995), and Fox News (since 2004). The database also includes special news broadcasts of political conventions, presidential speeches, and press conferences, Watergate hearings, coverage of the Persian Gulf War, the events of September 11, 2001, the War in Afghanistan, and the War in Iraq.

Fox News

http://www.foxnews.com/

Another news service that is popular throughout the country.

RELIGION

Association of Religious Data Archives (ARDA)

http://www.thearda.com/

ARDA "strives to democratize access to the best data on religion. Founded as the American Religion Data Archive in 1997 and going online in 1998, the initial archive was targeted at researchers interested in American religion." Since 1998, the database has been expanded in both audience and data collection now including American and international collections and developing features for educators, journalists, religious congregations, and researchers. "Contributors to the data included in the ARDA include the foremost religion scholars and research centers in the world. This database is currently housed in the Social Science Research Institute, the College of Liberal Arts, and the Department of Sociology at the Pennsylvania State University."

Bible Browser Online

http://www.biblebrowser.com/

This offers extremely thorough coverage of the Bible. You can select the language or the version you want to see and can also select portions of the Bible to explore.

TRANSPORTATION AND TRAVEL

Amtrak

http://www.amtrak.com/servlet/ContentServer?pagename=Amtrak/HomePage

Amtrak, the nation's intercity passenger rail services, connects the United States "in safer, greener and healthier ways. With 21,000 route miles in 46 states, the District of Columbia and three Canadian provinces, Amtrak operates more than 300 trains each day—at speeds up to 150 mph—to more than 500 destinations." Amtrak is the choice "for state-supported corridor services in 15 states and for four commuter rail agencies." This database provides fact sheets, documents and information about Amtrak's trains, corridors, improvement efforts, etc.

Hotelguide.com

http://www.hotelguide.com/home.seam

For the aspiring travel agent or a faculty member booking a tour for a university group, this database offers a broad selection of hotels, flights, car rentals, and shop-solutions worldwide at extremely competitive rates. It includes more than 120,000 hotels worldwide. Their primary target groups are corporate and leisure travelers and they offer selections from the world's leading brands including the following Web sites: hotels.com, hotel.de, priceline.com, travelweb.com, activehotels, booking.com, WorldRes, Sabre, Worldspan, and Pegasus.

The flight segment has a selection of over 2,000,000 international flight connections with the best fares. They also provide a selection of regular, low-cost, and charter flights. Their car rental segments guarantee the best available service at exclusive rates and includes both top international and well-recognized car rental companies as well as some local car rental agencies. The Shop-Solution segment offers one-stop-shop booking solutions with a comprehensive range of offers in the various travel segments. On this Website, a trip to any destination is completed in one single step.

ITA Software Fare Finder

http://www.itasoftware.com/

MIT computer science graduates founded ITA Software in the mid-1990s and they have pioneered a new generation of travel technology. Their world-class engineers and travel industry experts solved and continue to solve the industry's most complex computing challenges. Their software is used by some of the world's most successful travel companies, including American Airlines, Southwest Airlines, United Airlines, Continental Airlines, Bing, Kayak, and Orbitz.

Outdoor Travel Guides

http://www.gorp.com/

Away.com is a brand of The Away Network and is designed for travelers who want to choose their next vacation. Ideas and recommendations for trips are customized to specific travel interests. This database has more than two million pages of content covering nearly 50,000 destinations worldwide and offers a distinctive blend of expert and consumer advice. The Away Network itself includes Trip.com, a travel research site that allows its customers to quickly compare prices on multiple travel booking sites to find the best value. Another site, GORP.com, is the place for outdoor enthusiasts to plan hiking, camping, and visits to U.S. National Parks. It is focused on vacations both in the United States and worldwide. AdventureFinder.com is a directory of adventure vacations and outdoor-focused resorts while Outside Online is the website of *Outside*, the leading active lifestyle magazine in the United States.

Tourism Offices Worldwide Directory

http://www.towd.com/

"The Tourism Offices Worldwide Directory is your guide to official tourist information sources: government tourism offices, convention and visitors bureaus, chambers of commerce, and similar organizations that provide free, accurate, and unbiased travel information to the public. Businesses such as travel agents, tour operators, and hotels are not included." While using this Web site, keep in mind that many countries see themselves as tourist meccas, a view that we would not necessarily agree with.

U.S. National Park Service

http://www.nps.gov/findapark/index.htm

"Since 1916, the American people have entrusted the National Park Service with the care of their national parks. With the help of volunteers and park partners, we are proud to safeguard these nearly 400 places and to share their stories with more than 275 million visitors every year." Native American tribes, local governments, nonprofit organizations, businesses, and individual citizens use the site to help them revitalize their communities, preserve local history, celebrate local heritage, and create close to home opportunities for families to get outside, be active, and have fun.

Aircraft Licenses and Certificates

http://www.faa.gov/licenses_certificates/

This database includes information about Aircraft Certification, Airline Certification, Airmen Certification, Airport Certification, Commercial Space

Transportation, and Medical Certification. While high school students may be less interested in what it takes to become a licensed pilot, many adults who are thinking about flying as a hobby would be happy to access this Web site at their public library.

Airnav Airport Information

http://www.airnav.com/airports/

Detailed information is obtained after any one of several search methods.

Happy Landings 2011

http://www.landings.com/

This database includes just about everything you or your users would want or need to know about aviation such as flight planning, flight training, and information about general aviation.

National Transportation Safety Board

http://www.ntsb.gov/default.htm

This wide-range of databases deals with all aspects of transportation safety, not just aviation safety. Unfortunately, it can also be a scary site as one examines transportation disasters and incidents while browsing.

GEOGRAPHY AND MAPS

Earth View

http://www.fourmilab.ch/cgi-bin/uncgi/Earth/action?opt=-p

This Web site offers maps of the Earth showing the day and night regions at a single moment in time. You can also view the Earth from the Sun, the Moon, the night side of the Earth, above any location on the planet specified by latitude, longitude, and altitude. Views can be requested from a satellite in Earth orbit, or above various cities around the globe. These images "can be generated based on a full-color image of the Earth by day and night, a topographical map of the Earth, up-to-date weather satellite imagery, or a composite image of cloud cover superimposed on a map of the Earth, a color composite which shows clouds, land and sea temperatures, and ice, or the global distribution of water vapor." Their "expert mode" gives users additional control over the generation of the image. Custom requests can be generated with frequently-used parameters and saved as a hotlist or bookmark items in your browser.

Google Earth

http://earth.google.com

"Google Earth displays satellite images of varying resolution of the Earth's surface, allowing users to see things like cities and houses looking perpendicularly down or at an oblique angle (see also bird's eye view)." Google Earth's degree of available resolution is based somewhat on the points of interest and popularity; however, most land (except for some islands) is covered in at least 15 meters of resolution. The highest resolutions at 15 centimeters (6 inches) is found for Melbourne, Victoria, Australia; Las Vegas, Nevada, and Cambridge, England. This database also allows users to search for addresses for some countries, enter coordinates, or simply use the mouse to browse to a location. Students would be interested in seeing what their homes look like from the air. Enterprising U.S. history teachers might interest their students in comparing one of the Sanborn Insurance maps which were created in the twentieth century to the Google Earth images of those blocks of cities and towns at present.

Bing Maps

http://www.bing.com/maps/

Bing maps offers users topographically-shaded street maps for many cities worldwide including certain points of interest such as metro stations, stadiums, hospitals, and other facilities as well as public user-created points of interest. "Searches can cover public collections, businesses or types of business, locations, or people. There are 5 primary types of street map views available to users: Road View, Aerial View, Bird's Eye View, StreetSide View, and 3D View."

GOS: Geospatial One-Stop

http://gos2.geodata.gov

"Your One Stop for Finding and Using Geographic Data, Geodata.gov will help you:

- Find Data or Map Services
- Make a Map
- Browse Community Information
- Cooperate on Data Acquisitions
- Publish your Data and Map Services."

Users may save searches and maps to use again later. To open these personalization options, one must open the registration form.

Road Construction Database

http://corporate.randmcnally.com/rmc/tools/roadConstructionSearch.jsp?cmty=0

Are you tired of those orange cones which block your drive to school, work, etc.? This database will identify construction projects so you can avoid them. Unfortunately, it is not always completely up-to-date.

Terra Server

http://www.terraserver.com/

"TerraServer has assembled the largest variety of aerial photos, satellite images, oblique imagery and USGS topo maps on the Internet. You can search and view all of our online imagery and then purchase digital image downloads and high quality prints/posters." Some services have a fee for use, such as obtaining print maps.

National Geographic Online Maps

http://maps.nationalgeographic.com/maps

This database contains maps from the National Geographic Society. They include atlas maps, dynamic maps, and basic country facts.

LAW RESOURCES

National Criminal Justice Reference Service (NCJRS)

http://www.ncjrs.gov/App/search/AdvancedSearch.aspx

This database offers a range of services and resources that balance information needs with the ability of the technology to receive and access support. The following highlights a number of NCJRS services and resources: "NCJRS offers extensive reference and referral services to help you find answers to your questions about crime and justice-related research, policy, and practice. Search Questions & Answers to access hundreds of questions related to juvenile and criminal justice, victim assistance, drug policy, and NCJRS services." The site would be of value to those doing research on the juvenile justice system or for teachers using the information in their classes.

Federal Justice Statistics Program Resource Guide

http://www.icpsr.umich.edu/NACJD/fjsp/

"The Bureau of Justice Statistics (BJS) provides comprehensive information on suspects and defendants processed in the federal criminal justice system.

Federal agencies provide extracts from their case management systems, which cover various stages of criminal case processing." Because criminal justice is one of those hot new occupations, this would be of particular interest to college professors teaching in that field and to students (and other users) who enjoy TV crime dramas.

FindLaw: Case and Codes, Supreme Court Opinions

http://www.findlaw.com/casecode/supreme.html#dirsearch3

"FindLaw's searchable database of the Supreme Court decisions since 1893 (U.S. Supreme Court Decisions: U.S. Reports 150–, 1893–). Browsable by year and U.S. Reports volume number, and searchable by citation, case title and full text. We also maintain an archive of Opinion Summaries from September 2000 to the Present."

FindLaw Base Page

http://www.findlaw.com/

"FindLaw, a Thomson Reuters business, is the world's leading provider of online legal information and Internet marketing solutions for law firms. Find-Law's roots go back to 1995, when two attorneys compiled a list of Internet resources for a group of law librarians in northern California." When the response to this material was so positive, the developers decided to post the information on the Internet. Today, this database is one of the most popular sites for free legal information available on the Internet with more than 4,000,000 visitors each month. FindLaw has the largest legal directory available.

Legal Information Institute: Cornell University Law School

http://www.law.cornell.edu/

"We are a not-for-profit group that believes everyone should be able to read and understand the laws that govern them, without cost. We carry out this vision by:

• Publishing law online, for free.
• Creating materials that help people understand law.
• Exploring new technologies that make it easier for people to find the law."

Conclusion

Upon completing this book about the Invisible Web, I was suddenly struck by a thought that was at once both scary and thought-provoking: why should anyone, or more particularly any librarian, care about the Invisible Web? All around us all types of information professionals-academic, public, special, and school librarians-are being hamstrung or even eliminated by funding cutbacks at the national, state, and local levels. Too often, funding for library resources as well as personnel is being reduced or cut totally from the budget. We are all fighting for one piece of a rapidly diminishing pie.

Could the Invisible Web and the wealth of information available to Invisible Web users be used as a tool by budget-strapped administrators such as school boards, trustees, and legislators to threaten professional librarians in all arenas with the loss of their jobs? After all, it was not too many years ago when a member of a school board in my local area stated that school librarians and school libraries would soon not be needed because all the information students needed was available on the Internet and, best of all from his point of view, it was free. In a few locations, new institutions were built without that building or that room in the plans. However, once the institution was opened it became clear that an information facility really was necessary.

Many administrators question the purchase of commercial databases with their annual subscription fees. They think that free resources can replace fee-based ones. In many states, the cost of maintaining a state-wide database for users in all types of libraries is being scrutinized and funds are being cut from state budgets to fund them. In some cases, it has been the lack of statistics showing the beneficial use of these commercial databases to the advantage of student learning. In other cases, these commercial databases appear to be something that is considered to be a frill.

The question of why information professionals/librarians are needed in light of the proliferation of the Internet has been widely discussed in the library literature.Unfortunately, few in the administration of universities, city government, school districts, or corporations read library literature and, if it is brought to their attention by their librarians, they often view it as partisan propaganda.

The more anyone thinks about librarians knowing about the Invisible Web and helping their patrons use it, the less we need be concerned. Librarians in all types of libraries have little to fear in the use of the Invisible Web; their challenge is the increasing use of unchecked online resources such as the widespread "Googleitis." It is not educationally sound to think about replacing all other library resources with unfettered Internet access. Even unsophisticated searches with standard search engines such as Google can yield thousands of hits with only a few directly related to the topic and no assurance that any of the hits are authoritative, relevant, or accurate. Administrators may far underestimate the ability of their students and perhaps, even their sophistry. Students may be able to send text messages with great speed, but confirming a fact found on the Internet will be much slower and much less interesting to them. While these administrators do care about their students and their faculty, at the same time they are feeling increasingly threatened by financial realities.

This brings us back to the question I posed at the beginning of this conclusion: why should academic, public, school, or special librarians care about the Invisible Web and why should they encourage their clients to use it? The answer is relatively simple: it gives librarians another tool in their arsenal to fight what we could call "information ignorance." Information ignorance can be insidious. It can be a teacher telling students not to bother citing sources in a paper because citing rules are outmoded and too hard to learn. It can be our administrators who think all information formerly in libraries is now on the Internet and is, best of all, free. Most frightening of all is the fewer numbers of librarians who can help students who have used technology most or all of their lives learn not to be completely satisfied with Google searches. Someone needs to point out to students that within the millions of hits which may not be useful, they need to be looking for a few good and credible sources.

The answer to curing information ignorance thus becomes clearer; it is a task for the librarian. Students must be taught good, solid information literacy skills. Use the Invisible Web as a tool to help students find complete, accurate resources. Do not allow your students to be satisfied using only the Visible Web. It is incumbent on all of us to provide our students with the skills to search and retrieve the best sources to satisfy their information needs. This includes print resources (how soon we forget!), Visible Web resources, and, as mentioned throughout this book, Invisible Web resources. This is like a three-legged stool; if one element (leg of the stool) is eliminated, the stool cannot stand.

My charge to librarians who choose this book because they want to learn about the Invisible Web is threefold: first, you need to become proficient in searching and finding resources on the Invisible Web. Second, you must instruct your students in the efficient use of the Invisible Web. Third, you must convince your teachers that Google is not the "be-all and end-all" of Internet searching, but that the Invisible Web can help them and their students avoid information ignorance.

Bibliography

Bergman, Michael K. "White Paper: The Deep Web: Surfacing Hidden Value."
    August 2001. http://dx.dol.org/10.3998/3336451.0007.104 (accessed
    January 28, 2011).

Devine, Jane, and Francine Egger-Sider. *Going Beyond Google: The Invisible
    Web in Learning and Teaching.* New York: Neal-Schuman, 2009.

He, Bin, Mitesh Patel, Zhen Zhang, and Kevin Chen-Chaun Chang. "Accessing
    the Deep web." *Communications of the ACM* 50.5 May 2007:95–101.

Henninger, Maureen. *The Hidden Web: Finding Quality Information on the Net.*
    N.p.: UNSW Press, 2008.

Hock, Randolph. *The Extreme Searcher's Internet Handbook: A Guide for the
    Serious Searcher.* Medford, NJ: CyberAge Books, 2008.

Lackie, Robert J. "Those Dark Hiding Places: The Invisible Web Revealed."
    http://library.rider.edu/scholarly/rlackie/Invisible/Inv_Web.html
    (accessed January 28, 2011).

Lackie, Robert J. "The Evolving "Invisible Web": Tried-and-True Methods and
    New Developments for Locating the Web's Hidden Content." *College and
    Undergraduate Libraries.* 10.2 (2001): 65–70. http://www.haworthpress
    .com/store/product.asp?sku=j106 (accessed January 28, 2011).

McLaughlin, Laurianne. "Beyond Google." *PCWorld* (April 2004). http://
    www.pcworld.com (accessed January 28, 2011).

Mardis, Marcia. "Uncovering the Hidden Web, Part I: Finding What the Search
    Engines Don't." ERIC. http://www.eric.ed.gov/PDFS/ED456863.pdf
    (accessed January 28, 2011).

Mardis, Marcia. "Uncovering the Hidden Web, Part II: Resources for Your
    Classroom." ERIC. http://www.eric.ed.gov/PDFS/ED456864.pdf
    (accessed January 28, 2011).

Rosenfeld, Esther, and David V. Loertscher, ed. *Toward a 21st-Century School Library Media Program*. Lanham, MD, Scarecrow Press, 2007.

"Research Beyond Google: 119 Authoritative, Invisible, and Comprehensive Resources." http://oedb.org/library/college-basics/research-beyond -google (accessed January 28, 2011).

Sauers, Michael P. *Searching 2.0*. New York: Neal-Schuman, 2009.

Sherman, Chris, and Gary Price. *The Invisible Web: Uncovering Information Sources Search Engines Can't See*. Medford, NJ: Information Today, 2007.

Wright, Alan. "Searching the Deep Web." *Communications of the ACM* 51.10 Oct. 2008: 14–15.

Index

About the Author

William O. Scheeren is a Lecturer in Education at St. Vincent College, Latrobe, PA. He was formerly the Director of School Libraries in the Hempfield Area School District, Latrobe, PA, and holds a PhD from the University of Pittsburgh. Dr. Scheeren is also the author of *Technology for the School Librarian*.

Edwards Brothers, Inc.
Thorofare, NJ USA
March 20, 2012